# The Novels of Ruth Jhabvala and Anita Desai

*for*

my beloved mother, with so much love

# The Novels of Ruth Jhabvala and Anita Desai

M.A. WAHEED

Prestige

*an international publishing house*

*Published by*
**Prestige Books**
C 3/1, Janakpuri
New Delhi 110 058
Ph. 25507139, 9818755529
email: prestigebooks@gmail.com
website: www.asiabookclub.com



Printed at Chaman Offset Press, New Delhi 110 002

# Contents

# Abbreviations

*A Note on the Texts*

For the titles of Ruth Prawer Jhabvala's novels and Anita Desai's novels, where necessary, the following abbreviations have been used:

R.P. Jhabvala's Novels:

| | |
|---|---|
| *H* | *The Householder* |
| *GRB* | *Get Ready for Battle* |
| *EI* | *Esmond in India* |
| *BP* | *A Backward Place* |
| *HD* | *Heat and Dust* |

Anita Desai's Novels:

| | |
|---|---|
| *CP* | *Cry, the Peacock* |
| *VC* | *Voices in the City* |
| *WSGS* | *Where Shall We Go This Summer?* |
| *FM* | *Fire on the Mountain* |
| *IC* | *In Custody* |

# Preface

The study is based on the women's basic problems of survival and existence which have discovered new ways to counter the various forms of oppression meted to women in a male dominated society. The modern Indian woman writer in English after the second world war created an authentic treatment of the problems of man-woman relationship in terms of marital discord. The post-independence Indian scene also gushed forth like a stream, with force and velocity in different domestic issues like marital discord and in response to it the novelists viz. Jhabvala and Anita Desai have favourably responded to the changed situations like living in a psychologically tense, socially dynamic and economically uncertain milieu which is obviously not conducive to the establishment of interpersonal relationship. Certain clashes like East West encounter, traditionalism with modernism, socio-economic issues, cross-cultural tensions, psycho-political and social issues, clashes in systems and customs also contributed a lot to the issue of marital discord.

Therefore, Jhabvala and Anita Desai have come out in their fiction with an idea that despite radical changes in our society, people have to trust the concept of a happy, life-long marriage which is characterized by love and understanding besides efforts and commitments on the part of the spouse to maintain their marital relationship. In the context of Indian culture, marital bonds assume great significance since the familial ties are considered sacred in our country. All successful and satisfying bonds are based on a spirit of sacrifice and self-denial as the person with such bands does his duty ungrudgingly.

This book is divided into five chapters. The introductory chapter seeks to show how Indian English women novelists emerged with Indian English literary scene during the last quarter of the nineteenth century and showed great promise. It is significant in itself, marking the birth of a new era of the Indian women for dynamic participation in the social life of the country. Besides an overview of the Indian English women novelists, the description of man-woman relationship in terms of the great Indian English women novelists, the concept of "New Woman" and her identity is exposed. Jhabvala focuses the impact of diverse socio-economic problems for the flow of primary ties whereas Desai explores bonds from a psychologist's point of view. In this chapter, five novels of each author are taken up for the theme of marital discord. Besides, the summary of other seven novels of Jhabvala and other five novels of Desai are presented in short as extra information to the reader.

The second chapter deals with the study of Jhabvala's five novels which are rooted in the clash between orthodox tradition of the Indian society and modernity, between materialism and idealism and finally the East-West encounter. Automatically, these things led to marital discord.

The third chapter is devoted to Desai's five novels with the focus to study woman as a full human being and to treat her like a human being which will definitely help the man and woman to understand each other. The casual attitude of man towards woman should disappear in conjugal life, making way for peaceful life. This chapter deals with the problem of frustration in woman besides other related issues.

The fourth chapter deals with a comparative study between the fiction of Jhabvala and Desai. This study points out that there is divergence in the treatment of marital discord between Jhabvala and Desai. Jhabvala treats the theme with the keener awareness of the domestic, social, cultured, economic and philosophical implications but Desai probes the influence of these factors on the psyche of the protagonists. She pleads for the liberation of woman from the patriarchal oppression.

The fifth chapter offers the main theme of the thesis that Jhabvala and Desai have scientifically, systematically and effectively dealt with the theme of marital discord by projecting socio-economic and psychological aspects. It shows how the theme of marital discord erupts and how it can be solved systematically by taking the help of psychology, philosophy, religion and traditional history since traditional way of life taught patience, tolerance, sacrifice and adjustments. It is true that man is rigid and also it is true that woman is abnormal in her behaviour. This clue of thought should be dealt carefully at least to live long and peacefully better.

**M.A. WAHEED**

## Acknowledgements

I take this opportunity to express my deep sense of indebtedness and gratitude to all those who helped me in bringing out this book on the fiction of Jhabvala and Anita Desai: A study in the theme of Marital Discord. I am grateful to Dr. A.G. Khan, Professor, Department of English and Director, Board of Colleges and University Development, Dr. Babasaheb Ambedkar Marathwada University, Aurangabad (Maharashtra) for his insightful comments and critical remarks which went a long way in shaping this book. I am grateful to Professor V. Sasikumar, formerly, Head, Department of Material Production and Dean of Studies, CIEFL, Hyderabad; Professor Siddique Ali, Director, Academic Staff College, Osmania University, Hyderabad; Professor D. Kanak Durga, Department of English, Osmania University, Hyderabad; Prof. M. Rajagopalachary, Principal, UPGC, Kakatiya University, Nirmal; Mr. L.S. Ramaiah, formerly Librarian, CIEFL, Hyderabad; who have helped me as and when I approached them.

But for the loving concern of my mother Mahaboob Begum, my brother M.A. Moin, my daughters Sana Waheed and Saba Waheed and my son M.A. Moyeed, it would not have been possible for me to undertake this project. I fondly remember and acknowledge their help. I am deeply beholden to my loving wife, Khaleda Khatoon, Gazetted Head Mistress, Zilla Parishad Secondary School, Angadichittampally, Rangareddy District, Andhra Pradesh, but for whose initiative and drive, affectionate care and constant encouragement I would not have been in a position to complete the book. I remain indebted to her forever.

**M.A. WAHEED**

Chapter I

# Introduction
## Indian English Women Novelists: An Overview

Indian English literature in the recent past has attracted widespread interest both in India and abroad. The most powerful form of creative expression in Indian English literature is obviously fiction. Being the most characteristic and powerful form of literary expression, fiction has acquired a prestigious position in Indian English literature. As a distinct literary form, the novel will be truly representative of a total response to Indian English literature. Lal Behari Day's *Govinda Samanta* (1874) is established as the first significant Indian English novel while Bankim Chandra Chatterji's *Rajmohan's Wife,* though chronologically an earlier work considering its appearance in a serial form in *The Indian Field* of 1864, came out in book form as late as 1935. *Rajmohan's Wife,* which is typical of a transitional period in the history of Indian English literature, was the first attempt made by an Indian to produce a novel in English, but it does not illustrate all the aspects of the rise of the novel in India as does *Govinda Samanta.*

Women novelists appeared on the Indian English literary scene during the last quarter of the nineteenth century (1874-1900) and showed great promise. The emergence of women writing in English during this period was quite significant in itself, marking the birth of a new era which held out for the Indian woman opportunities for dynamic participation in the social life of the country. While the rise of the novel in India in English was a symptom of the emergence of the individualistic social order, the contribution made to the rise of the Indian English novel by women at its first phase, by writers like Toru Dutt, Shevanti Bai Nikambe, Krupabai Sathianathan, Cornelia Sorabji, Swarna-kumari Ghosal and others made the phenomenon an instrument of social reform and regeneration.

Writings of these women novelists of the first phase are to be seen in terms of Indian feminine sensibility with certain emotional and aesthetic propensities and predilections shared by the Indian English women writers even today. It should be admitted, however, that the attempt of many of the early women novelists was to locate their problems in the male-dominated society. They also turned to didacticism, sentimentalism and romanticism. The second phase of women writers witnessed the emergence of the new woman in the fast-changing social milieu waiting for liberation from the tyranny of the ages. They offer a convincing world in which characters live with maturity. They forge a style and project a vision of their own. They reveal a power of artistic selection by which their novels tend to achieve harmony. The recurring theme of many of the Indian English novels is quest for woman's identity and self-awareness. The post-Independence Indian scene, with rapid criss-cross socio-political changes has stimulated a variety of reactions in Indian English women writers. The fervour and expression, uptil now, lying under the ashes of the unextinguished earth was set ablaze violently after Independence and shone with brightness. The pent-up emotions gushed forth like a stream, with force and velocity in different channels and directions. It is noteworthy that critical works, domestic issues, marital problems, and feministic outbursts appeared only after Independence. The feelings of protest and frustration found full expression in the modern age. The women novelists however seem to have favourably responded to the changed situations, psychological realities, the phenomenal attainment of freedom in a spirit of analytical reconstruction of Indian life.

The modern Indian woman writer in English with reference to the basic problem of survival and existence, discovered new ways to counter the various forms of oppression meted out to women in a male-dominated society. The female protagonists in the novels of writers of the second phase are no revolutionaries, but in order to survive, they successfully create a niche for themselves. They were more concerned with the minutia of everyday existence besides their struggle to keep up their ideology and identity. Their suffering was mental, emotional, social, psychological and existential. They seem to have been guided by the age-old experience of repression of Indian women. Kamala Markandaya, Ruth Prawer Jhabvala, Attia Hosain, Nayantara Sahgal, Anita Desai, Bharati Mukherjee, Shashi Deshpande, Nargis Dalal, Rama Mehta, Shanta Rama Rau, Shobha De, Veena Paintal, Mrinalani Sarabhai, Jai Nimbkar and Shouri Daniels, who constitute this group are emotionally and intellectually equipped to offer an authentic fictional treatment of the problems of man-woman relationship in terms of marital dissonance, socio-cultural issues, socio-political and socio-economic problems. In the novels of these writers, there is a welcome shift in the focus of the themes of psycho-social issues, and the prevalent critical tendency to attach the tag of sociological and psychological fiction to their work is quite disconcerting.

It is only after the Second World War that women novelists of quality have begun enriching Indian fiction in English. These prominent and eminent women novelists, inspired by the feminist movement in the West, accepted the statement of Virginia Woolf: "there is the obvious and enormous difference of experience in the first place; but the essential difference lies in the fact not that men describe battles and women the birth of the children, but that each sex describes itself."[1] Emotionally, it is a natural gift for women novelists to expose themselves to their own problems more insightfully. Vimala Rao explains this gift very articulately:

> Women, by nature, see, hear and talk more exuberantly than the men. Being at the centre of the vanities of life nothing escapes them. Keen observation, a quick perception, a fine sensibility and

> an intuitive insight into life are the strong points of any novelist. Women novelists have made use of some of these natural gifts in the writing of their novels.[2]

There is the charge of narrowness and lack of vision against women novelists in general. But Indian English women novelists stand as a unique exception to this rather sweeping generalisation. The personal background and intellectual training of these novelists seem to have endowed the specialty which their fictional product bears. Their wide acquaintance with the vagaries and nuances of life, both in the East and the West, and their achievement of often high educational and intellectual standards have given a sharp edge to their observations. Their natural feminine sensibility and introspection have imparted to their observation a humane touch and a psychological depth and to their art a neat finish and precision of outline. The new material of life they have seized upon and transformed into art has remained faithful to life in its changed form, relegating didactic, sociological, psychological and philosophical concerns to a place of marginal importance. Consequently man-woman relationship has assumed tremendous importance in their fiction.

## II

From the very beginning of human life, an individual is placed in the midst of a group of people—his kin, whom he has not chosen. In the process of growing up, one encounters new faces and personalities and the interaction goes on forever. No matter how autonomous and how strong one's personality is, the commonly-shared norms, beliefs and practices of the kin group mould the individual. The interaction between the group and the individual is sometimes negative and sometimes positive. At times, it provides one an opportunity to enjoy happiness, fulfillment and a sense of identity, whereas on other occasions it causes only disillusionment and a feeling of alienation. As David Krech observes: "Insofar as we can tease out the separate influences of the individual's personality and the forces of the group we find that sometimes group membership inhibits man, constricts his creativity, and prevents self-fulfilment. But also find that sometimes the individual can best express his individuality and can most fully develop his originality with the security of his own group."[3]

The most intimate interactions are possible in primary groups which imply "two or more persons in intimate, face to face association. The most important primary groups are the family, friendship and work groups. They are primary in the sense of their enduring influence upon the individual."[4] Family is man's immediate fragment of society. "For man does not live in cosmos, he lives in microcosm."[5] Contrary to the belief about primitive promiscuity and sexual communism, the immediate family is not, everywhere and at all times, set apart as sharply as it is in our culture, but it is recognised nonetheless. As a psychological group, the family is significant as in its structure are involved three fundamental bonds: the marital, parental and sibling. Even this small group, simple as it may seem, offers challenging possibilities of complex ties. Notwithstanding our weaknesses and strengths, predilections and aversions, we all are influenced and constrained by family relationships. The important institution besides family is marriage. Whereas all the other animals enter into mating relationships, human beings go through a procedure of marriage to establish a family. "Marriage in the biological sense is a sexual relationship entered into with the intention of making it permanent, even apart from whether or not it has sanction of law or the church."[6] Therefore, as Alexander Walker says: "History proves that marriage is essential to the well being of human society and that celibacy brings ruins upon states."[7] In most societies throughout the world, marriage is considered a permanent life-long and sacred union. "In spite of all these dicta and slogans supporting the indissolubility of marriage, there are factors, internal as well as external, working to undermine the stability of marital ties. Such a situation is termed 'marital dissonance' which may be manifested in various forms, divorce being the final."[8]

The primary ties within the family fold are universally esteemed and cherished. Nevertheless, in the modern age these fundamental bonds have become fragile under the pressure of inbuilt personality traits, a quest for identity, external stresses, economic and political upheavals. Despite several common qualities, each human being is a living affirmation of the ubiquity of individual differences. Consequently, temperamental properties influence even basic human relationships.

In the rich stratum of Indian society the institutions of marriage and family have come under tremendous strain in modern times. One of the major causes of the disintegration of a family is the rampant promiscuity in sexual relations. Another factor is the lack of a set routine of work and excessive leisure among women of the richer classes which becomes "a chief cause of the restless, exacting, often historical spirit harassing to the owner and everyone else, which tends towards discontent, indiscretion and divorce."[9] Subhash Chandra finds the new definition of marriage which "postulates complete sexual freedom, with no notion of marital fidelity."[10]

Despite radical changes in our society, most people still favour a happy, life-long marriage characterised by love and understanding. Some would see the perfect relationship as a merger of two selves, "a marriage of two minds." This is, however, something really unattainable. In fact, people can fall out of love, remain locked in unhappy marriages or seek divorce. One of the problems is that situations change and people change. It requires effort and commitment on the part of the spouses to maintain their marital relationship.

Besides the psychological attributes, external circumstances also affect mutual ties. These concern the mundane realities of human existence: the economic stresses, political tension and the changes in the value-system of the society. Continuous adjustments and consistent adaptations are required and must be accomplished to accommodate the diversity of external influences. The solidarity and strength of a relationship is seen in terms of its ability to absorb such stresses through internal, interactional and sequential modifications.

In the context of Indian culture, marital and filial bonds assume great significance since familial ties are considered sacred in our country. All relationships—whether matrimonial, filial or sibling—are based on the idea of doing one's duty ungrudgingly. All successful and satisfying bonds are based on a spirit of sacrifice and self-denial. However, the changed temperament of the age, when a distinctly individual identity is the cherished dream of every individual, has dealt a severe blow to the traditional concept of primary relationships. These ties are being seen from a different perspective altogether. Subtle cultural and intellectual changes, responsible for a shift in emphasis, from a collective destiny to an individual identity, are causing great upheaval in the psychic ecology of the contemporary man. Modern man is therefore living in a psychologically tense, socially dynamic and economically uncertain milieu which is obviously not conducive to the establishment and development of gratifying interpersonal relationships.

## III

The portrayal of man-woman relationship is as old as the novel itself. Samuel Richardson (1689-1761) and Henry Fielding (1707-1754) on the one hand and D.H. Lawrence (1885-1930), Virginia Woolf (1882-1941), Ernest Hemingway (1898-1961) and William Faulkner (1897-1962) on the other, have been primarily concerned with this fundamental relationship. As D.H. Lawrence points out: "The great relationship for humanity will always be the relation between man and woman."[11] This theme is popular with Indian English novelists as well. R.K. Narayan embodies the incompatible man-woman relationships in *The Dark Room* and *The Guide*, Raja Rao in *The Serpent and the Rope,* Mulk Raj Anand in *Gauri*, Bhabani Bhattacharya in *Music for Mohini*, Manohar Malgonkar in *A Bend in the Ganges,* Arun

Joshi in *The Foreigner* and *The Strange Case of Billy Biswas,* Kamala Markandaya in *The Coffer Dams*, Ruth Prawer Jhabvala in *Heat and Dust*, Anita Desai in *Cry, the Peacock*, Nayanatara Sahgal in *This Time of Morning,* Shashi Deshpande in *That Long Silence* and Bharati Mukherjee in *Wife*.

In R.K. Narayan's *The Guide*, the husband-wife relationship disintegrates because of the temperamental and attitudinal differences between Rosy and Marco. The narrative pattern of Anita Desai's *Cry, the Peacock* resembles that of *The Guide* with the difference that while Raju in the latter stage of the novel develops consciousness by renouncing the will to live the kind of life he has been living and thereby achieves salvation in this life itself, Maya fails to develop this consciousness and as a consequence kills her husband before committing suicide.

The fiction of Indian women novelists of the second phase constitutes a major segment of contemporary Indian writing in English. It provides insights, a wealth of understanding, a reservoir of meanings and a basis of discussion in terms of man-woman relationship. In fact, in order to realise the potential human achievement in any appraisal of Indian English literature, an appreciation of the writing of its women is essential. Kamala Markandaya's vision has been often termed 'tragic'—a vision which compels her to rely on social realism and moral realism and to portray characters torn by conflicts such as tradition versus modernity and East versus West. To A.V. Krishna Rao, Markandaya's novels seem to be "more fully reflective of the awakened feminine sensibility in modern India as she attempts to project the image of the changing traditional society,"[12] the fictional focus in *A Silence of Desire* (1961) being "on the psychological adjustment of an urban middle class family."[13] Helen in Markandaya's *The Coffer Dams* (1969) and Olivia in Jhabvala's *Heat and Dust* (1975) are sensitive and emotional. Both are independent and dislike superficialities and conventions which mar their sense of fulfilment in life. Both are non-conformists and want to have their own way. Their inner force drives them to react vigorously when their husbands, Clinton and Douglas Rivers, treat them as objects or subordinates rather than as individuals. Olivia seeks solace in Nawab's company. Her affair results in pregnancy and rejection of Douglas, whereas Helen's affair, though it does not achieve fulfilment, leads her to liberation. The last meeting between Helen and Clinton is dramatic and suggestive, "Clinton and Helen stood face to face unable to achieve each other's views."[14]

Nayantara Sahgal is a spokeswoman of "new humanism" and "new morality, according to which a woman is not to be regarded as "a sex object and a glamour girl, fed on fake dreams of perpetual youth, lulled into a passive role that requires no individual identity"[15] but as a co-partner and an honoured companion of man. The humanist in her vouches for the need for unrestricted freedom because "human personality is a precious, hard-won achievement, worthy of nature, irrespective of sex."[16] She advocates a new and fresh exploration of man-woman relationship that still seems largely unresearched even in the atomic age when monumental problems have been explored and resolved. Her novels also explore and highlight the two themes: First, she sees India in transition and Indians adapting and adjusting them to those changes; and the second prominent theme is a lack of communication between individuals, specially husband and wife. She, therefore, desires and pleads for a truly mature and harmonious union between the sexes. The women in Sahgal's novels sometimes break the barriers and customs that prevent their emancipation and their lifestyles. In her novel, *This Time of Morning* (1965), Rashmi, the daughter of Kailas and Mira, is an antithesis to her mother. Whereas Mira is a steadfast loyal wife, embodying and exemplifying the myth of Sita and Savitri, Rashmi married to Rakesh, an I.F.S officer, believes in breaking off relations that do not work. Back in her parents' home, alienated and utterly disturbed, she gets a divorce and seeks extra-marital relationships, feeling a sense of release from ancient pain and suppression.

Shashi Deshpande, comparatively a recent entrant into the literary scene, portrays the new Indian woman and her dilemma in her novels. She concerns herself with the plight of the modern Indian woman trying to understand herself and to preserve her identity as wife, mother and above all as a human being. Such a quest for identity forms the theme of her Sahitya Akademi Award winning novel, *That Long Silence* (1989). Jaya, the protagonist, thinks of her past days and tries to analyse herself, "to decide who she really is."[17] The fact that Jaya was rechristened Suhasini by Mohan her husband, on their wedding day confuses Jaya in her search for identity. The pseudonym under which she operates as a writer further complicates the issue. Jaya stands for revolt whereas Suhasini symbolizes submission. Therefore, Jaya rejects her name—Suhasini. She seeks her individuality to be valued equally with that of man. But Jaya is confident of her individuality and hopeful of a change in Mohan's attitude. Such an optimistic ending of the novel shows that the day is not far off when men and women will be valued equally, ensuring unsullied dignity, individuality and self-respect to women.

Commenting on the achievement of Bharati Mukherjee, M. Sivaramakrishna underlines the portrayal of her protagonists as the "victims of life which is visionless because it is voiceless. Therefore, these characters are shown struggling to find modes of authentic communication."[18] Dimple's psychic troubles, especially her "impulse towards self-destruction," could be related to her inability to 'voice' the agony she 'scarcely understands.' Jasbir Jain observes that Bharati Mukherjee's characters suffer from 'isolation,' Dimple's being routed in her "estrangement from her own past and her own inner being."[19]

## IV

Ruth Prawer Jhabvala's writing career now spans forty years and she has so far produced twelve novels and five collections of short stories. She has been the recipient of a number of major awards and prizes. In 1975 her novel *Heat and Dust* won Britain's prestigious Booker Prize. She received John Simon Guggenheim Memorial Fellowship in 1976, Neil Gunn International Fellowship in 1979 and MacArthur Foundation award in 1986. Jhabvala's screenplay for Merchant-Ivory's film of E.M. Forster's novel *A Room with a View* won an Academy Award in 1987. Her screenplay for the Merchant-Ivory film of Forster's novel, *Howards End* won the Oscar Award in 1993.

Ruth Prawer Jhabvala was born in Cologne, Germany on 7th May 1927. Her father, Marcus Prawer, was a Polish-Jewish lawyer and her mother, Eleanora, though born in Cologne, was of Russian background. In 1939, Ruth Jhabvala and her family escaped from Nazi Germany and settled in England. Soon after graduating, she married Cyrus S.H. Jhabvala, an Indian architect at the age of twenty-four and went to live in India. In India, Jhabvala, as she somewhat cryptically signed herself, became a writer. Most of her novels and short stories were set in Delhi, though published in England and the United States, and intended for a Western audience.[20]

Her Indian fiction is spun by an "initiated outsider"—the phrase is John Updike's—working from within a domestic world.[21] If nothing else, the remarkable point of view elicits the comment: a Bombay literary headline hit upon a similar phrase, naming her "outsider with unusual insight."[22] This perspective was not available to any of the great Anglo-European novelists who have addressed themselves to cross-cultural issues: one thinks of the very different world of James, Forster and Conrad. For all their exotic settings, Jhabvala's novels of middle class Indian life present an incongruous but inescapable similarity to those of Jane Austen, since in many ways—the large family, strict codes of behaviour, constant presence of relations—that settings has more in common with 18th century England than it has with the modern West, as the writer has pointed out.[23] In an early interview, she admitted that "perhaps my way of looking at things may have been somewhat similar to hers—a sort of ironic detachment? May be."[24] As Gooneratne has observed "A close reading of Jhabvala's earliest novels reveals conscious allusion to *Pride and Prejudice.*"[25]

As a novelist Jhabvala's concern is to give a true picture of middle class society in urban India. She achieves her object by arranging incidents that throw light on the essential traits of her characters. In this respect, Jhabvala is also like the 19th century novelists, W.M. Thackeray (1811-1863) and Charles Dickens (1812-1870), who wrote what Edwin Muir calls "novels of character."

Jhabvala's writing career falls into three phases: the initial phase includes the first five novels from *To Whom She Will* to *Get Ready for Battle,* which are primarily concerned with Indian domestic and social problems; the second phase which includes *A Backward Place. A New Dominion* and *Heat and Dust*, sees a shift in interest from the predominantly Indian concerns of her earlier novels to a concern with the Europeans in India—reflecting Jhabvala's own heritage; and the third phase is that of her more recent 'American' novels. In this section, there are four novels from *In Search of Love and Beauty* to *Shards of Memory.*

Jhabvala views the game of human affairs in an Indian family from a point of view which is both objective and unsentimental. Her worldliness and down-to-earth approach to life indirectly aid her in avoiding the pitfalls of sentimentality or superficial involvement with varieties of Indian religious or mystical beliefs. Jhabvala's merit as a creative writer lies in her being intensely aware of her limitations. She writes about possibly the only social segment of urban India that she knows at first hand. In fact, she also delineates the rising commercial bourgeois which is by no means really sophisticated. She shows her awareness of the variety and complexity of the post-Independence Indian society. Her urban India is not urbane, in fact it can be described as a backwater. Her basic literary endeavour is to portray the human portent of this society caught in the conflict of a change from tradition to modernity. She also delineates the theme of East-West encounter in *Esmond in India* and *A Back-*

*ward Place* in the sense that Europeans are confronted with this inevitable situation of the Hindu joint families. Such of her interaction between two cultures is her special forte.

Jhabvala's world of alienation is primarily social. She deals with the situation of breakdown of a traditional social order thereby highlighting the alienation or isolation between one individual and another in marital relations, in family life, in the society at large. She also takes up the theme of materialism versus idealism in her *Get Ready for Battle*. Surprisingly, she explores the theme of East-West get-together for spiritual guides in India in her novel *A New Dominion.* The theme of marital dissonance is compellingly dealt with in five of her novels wherein the women characters are central figures.

Jhabvala's first novel *To Whom She Will* (1955) bears the central problem of the arranged versus the romantically-based marriage. H.M. Williams remarks that the theme of the novel is "loosely marriage in the context of modern family life in India."[26] Amrita Chakravarty, the young protagonist, has been brought up in an anglicized way by her grandfather Pandit Ram Bahadur Saxena, a retired English-educated lawyer who travelled throughout the world. She is the daughter of the late Nirad Chakravarty, a political idealist. Amrita in her pseudo-westernism romances with Hari Sahni, her colleague at the All India Radio. Hari is simple, unspoiled and traditional. Amrita and Sahni love each other and want to marry in spite of their conflicting ways. But Ram Bahadur disapproves of Amrita's love affair with Hari, who belongs to a different community with poor Punjabi refugee family background. Under the influence of her widowed mother Radha and her grandfather, Amrita relents and reconciles to the notion of marrying Krishna Sengupta, a Bengali lecturer. Hari is emotionally forced by the protective love of his old-fashioned parents to accept their proposal for an arranged marriage with Sushila, a pretty singer. Thus, ironically, both Amrita and Hari are married to partners arranged for them. Hari marries Sushila not for love but for social compromise. His sister Prema is afraid of Amrita's forward ways and the opulence of her mother, Radha. *To Whom She Will* thus ends on a note of reconciliation achieved through arranged marriages. Jhabvala, through this novel, reinforces the correctness of the institution of arranged marriage. As Ralph J. Crane observes, "it [the arranged marriage] asserts the solidity of the *household* and its ability to survive. Boundaries are not crossed. Communities are not split. Families are not divided. The household remains intact."[27] Jhabvala seems to suggest that the Indian society, though appears to be modern, is quite traditional and conservative.

The title of *The Nature of Passion* (1956), Jhabvala's second novel, is taken from the *Bhagvad Gita* where *rajas* nature, the worldly passion for pleasure, is described. The three modes such as *sattvika* (the saintly), *rajas* (the worldly) and *tamas* (the angry) are present in all human beings in different degrees. The chief protagonist, Lala Narayan Dass Verma—Lalaji—is corrupt but emperor of capital devoted to provide everything to the joint family. He has a passion to accumulate wealth and pursuit of wealth is his path of duty. His earthiness and worldliness are the result of his passion. Here Jhabvala focuses on the 'money-civilization' paradox of a rising commercial middle class family comprising Lalaji, his wife, sister, three sons, three daughters and two daughters-in-law. Lalaji's passion is threatened by the Westernized attitudes of his daughter Nimmi, sons Chandra Prakash and Viddi. Nimmi is against arranged marriages. She wants an open society and develops friendship with a Parsi playboy, Pheroze Batliwala. Lalaji's son Chandra has his education abroad and is married to an intellectual snob Kanta who detests everything about Lalaji's family. Viddi, the youngest son, takes pride in idling away his time in a cafe with pseudo-artists. His eldest son, Om, is like Lalaji, a hungry capitalist. Once Lalaji was involved in a great corruption scandal of offering bribes to obtain government contracts. His alienated son Chandra, a civil servant, extricates him. Lalaji clings to the old orthodox Hindu way, its rituals and customs, but his son Viddi and daughter

Nimmi move in free society. Like that of Amrita of *To Whom She Will*, Nimmi's marriage is arranged, but the husband chosen for her is not the Parsee boy but Viddi's friend, Kuku who is of her own religion and community. With his daughter's marriage, Lalaji's worries and anxieties are resolved.

In her third novel, *Esmond in India* (1958), Jhabvala deals with the theme of marital dissonance. There is a more direct clash between the Englishman Esmond and his Indian wife Gulab. Esmond scrapes by in India by giving private lessons in Hindi, Indian History and literature to English *memsahibs*, tourists and rich Indian sophisticates. The marital relationship between Esmond and Gulab deteriorates rapidly after the birth of a son Ravi, adored and spoilt by his mother Gulab and grandmother Uma. The marriage becomes a battlefield with Esmond trying to make Gulab bring Ravi up in the European way. But Gulab reverts to Indian ways in the absence of Esmond. Her mother begs Gulab to leave Esmond and come here. Esmond is cruel with Gulab, savagely sarcastic, pinching and slapping her but Gulab meekly surrenders accepting the traditional role of the Indian wife to whom the husband is a god. She resists leaving Esmond till the end of novel, disgusted and furious only after a servant tries to rape her during one of Esmond's protracted absences. She then blames Esmond for the attack and leaves him for good with her son. As Williams observes: "Jhabvala resolutely avoids making tragedy explicit or even implicit."[28] Again, the issue of marital dissonance surfaces in Jhabvala's fourth novel *The Householder* (1960). It is centred on the married life of Prem and his young wife Indu. The tale is told with gentle mocking irony. Prem teaches in a private college owned by the pompous Mr. Khanna and his even more odious wife. They do not pay their staff well but strive on the profits that the college fetches. Moreover, they treat their staff with scant respect. They are almost Dickensian in their comic awfulness. To Prem his role of a householder is seriously affected by his meagre resources.

To make matters worse, Prem's landlord Mr. Seigal threatens to raise the rent.

Prem is proudly conscious of his dignity as a lecturer and feels uncertainty and shame in his desire for his wife's body. He constantly recalls the fact that his father had been a college principal. Their marriage is an arranged one. He scarcely knows his wife and what he knows he dislikes and despises. Prem's bossy mother comes to live with them. The imposing presence of mother-in-law irritates Indu. The traditional problem of hostility between the mother-in-law and the daughter-in-law is highlighted in the novel. Indu wants her mother-in-law to go away. Prem, as the householder, fails to solve this problem with the result that Indu goes away to her mother. Temporarily, Prem feels happier but soon realises the importance of his wife for whom he buys a piece of pink satin. But his mother's possessiveness fills him with remorse so that he gives that piece to her to cheer her up. When Indu returns, he discovers the true value of his young wife. Therefore, he plans to send his mother to his sister and feels relieved when she leaves them. He does not wait to see the train leave and hurries back to his wife. The novel ends on Prem's discovery of his passionate love for his wife. The novel begins with dissonance but ends with coexistence.

In contrast to *Esmond in India*, the central character Sarla Devi in Jhabvala's fifth novel *Get Ready for Battle* (1962) is stubbornly saintly. She is a plain middle-aged woman who refuses to compromise with the new India which is full of the hypocrisy of the rich, cultured middle class Indians, do-gooders and money-lovers. Her husband Gulzari Lal is a rich Punjabi businessman who has largely adapted to Western manners of life though "he still liked to sit on the floor and eat his food from little bowls with his fingers" (*GRB*, 26). His concern is to improve his business deals by buying the land at *Bundi Busti* in Delhi for his economic gains through ousting the slum dwellers. On the contrary, Sarla Devi insists on pursuing ideals of justice as an obstinate reformer. The ideological differences between Gulzari

Lal and Sarla Devi create the base for disintegration and maladjustment in their married life. Her high principles and selfless behaviour with courageous temperament based on the teachings of Lord Krishna in the *Bhagvad Gita* and his low principles and selfish behaviour with demoralised temperament based on the moneymaking rules of modern society lead to marital dissonance. However, she finally consents to divorce Gulzari Lal. For she hopes to renew her spirits after every failure and plunges into a fresh mission to serve the poor in the red-light area.

Jhabvala has explored "the themes of expatriates in India and the mixed marriage of Indian and European."[29] Besides *Esmond in India*, her sixth novel, *A Backward Place* (1965), also portrays the various phases experienced by the Europeans in India. Esmond feels suffocated in the alien country India after the initial enthusiasm evaporates and he starts hating his wife. But Judy, in *A Backward Place*, succeeds in adopting herself to India and hence escapes the serious conflict, though both are different in their temperaments. Judy's husband Bal is irresponsible, irrepressible and believes in impracticable dreams. His attitude towards life is childish and unsteady. He dreams to become an actor in the film world of Bombay. In contrast, Judy is cautious, working, realistic to the core. She believes in pragmatism. She is mature and retains her Anglo-Saxon coolness. But these very qualities, instead of working as barriers to her coming closer to her people, help her to put up with Bal's impracticable optimism. This creates marital dissonance between them but her positive attitude to life helps her to accept the challenges of life. One can see that "the marriage of Bal and Judy is difficult not because of the difference in race so much as because of the clash in their temperaments between the dreamer and the pragmatist."[30] But Judy's love for Bal and her readiness to adapt and accept, help her to be happy and contented in the face of adversity and want too.

Jhabvala's seventh novel, *A New Dominion* (1972), explores the theme of east-west get-together for spiritual guides in India.

*A New Dominion* is contemporary India and her multifarious realities. This novel projects primarily the British and American view of contemporary India wherein the Indian traditional concept of spiritualism is diluted. Here in the novel, Jhabvala portrays the Western women and their attempt to grapple with the spiritual India. The Western characters are not in India to do good to the country but "to do good to themselves, to learn, to take from India."[31] Therefore, they surrender to India. Three girls—Lee, Margaret and Evie—come to India in search of spiritual truth and peace. Lee comes to India "to lose herself in order to find herself."[32] She wants to have a pure heart untainted by modern materialism. She comes to India as a revolt against her life at home and her family. Evie has been in India for three years with Swamiji and it is all she wants. While "Lee and Margaret seek a merging of their selves with that of the Swamiji, as a symbol of India's heritage of mysticism and spiritual glory, Evie is even more intensely identified with what she believes to be the soul of India as embodied in the Swamiji."[33] They come across a spurious Swamiji. The West turns to the East, not because it believes, trusts and admires the spirituality of the East, but to fill the vacuum in their lives. One cannot find fault with Jhabvala for the distorted picture of Swamiji, for India has no dearth of such fake Swamis. They look at Swamiji as a symbol of India's spirituality and seek complete identification with him. Hariprasanna observes: "the tragedy is that they do not know what they want, nor do they know where they can find it. They get confused between physical union and spiritual communion, therefore, they submit to the lust of Swamiji."[34]

Olivia of Jhabvala's eighth novel, *Heat and Dust* (1975), is a complete contrast to Judy of *A Backward Place*. Unlike Lee, Evie and Margaret in *A New Dominion*, Olivia and her husband Douglas are not on a spiritual quest. Olivia too suffers from marital dissonance as she has developed a critical attitude towards Douglas. She is a pretty young woman, rather vain, pleasure-seeking and a little petulant. She comes to India with Douglas whom she thinks she loves. But shortly after her arrival in India, she meets the Nawab, feels attracted towards him and has an affair with him. Though Olivia succeeds in keeping away the heat and dust of India by shutting all the doors and windows, she succumbs to the heat of passion in herself. She gets her pregnancy aborted for fear that the child would betray her to her husband. Therefore, she is forced to be isolated to live all alone on the hills of the Himalayas and later she dies there.

Jhabvala's ninth novel, *In Search of Love and Beauty* (1983), is set in New York. In this novel Jhabvala explores and unravels the tangled emotional web called love. Laurie Sucher rightly observes: "every protagonist in Jhabvala's fiction has been in search of love and beauty."[35] She also investigates the combination of spiritual longing and erotic obsession that her characters know as love. The characters presented in this novel are Leo Kellerman, Louise, Marietta, Regi and Natasha. Leo Kellerman is a German refugee psychiatrist who collects a devoted coterie to scrutinize their psyches. He knows how to exploit the vulnerable searchers after love and beauty who are mostly female. This novel examines the effects of this search on a group of German and Austrian refugees in New York and two generations of their descendants.

Leo establishes his "Academy for Potential Development," a sort of Western *ashram* catering to the "psychological needs" of dissatisfied woman who could no longer manage themselves and feel the need to hand themselves over to someone stronger. Leo is such a person with the powers of Adonis. Louise, who is attracted by his power takes him to her apartment and sleeps with him. Her friend Regi too is involved in such an affair separately. Besides this, Marianne, the daughter of Louise and Brunto, a Jew, renames herself as Marietta and marries Tim, but for her sexual pleasure she also sleeps with Leo. Leo's Gothic Academy, the large and dark mansion, connotes sexual love as the supreme point of adventure. Leo preaches that "impulses" must be satisfied. However, "the Academy is a cheap exploitation of the human search for love and beauty."[36] Meanwhile, Tim dies in an accident. His wife, Marietta, meets an Indian musician called Ahmed and develops an affair with him. Leo also meets Ahmed and incorporates Tantrism into his teaching. Such teachings provoke Marietta's adopted daughter Natasha and her son Mark. Natasha loves Mark and Mark develops a homosexual relationship with an Indian named Ravi during his visit to India. Thus, both the male homosexuals and the women heterosexuals in this novel are drawn towards the phallic desire for love and beauty which brings disaster to all.

Jhabvala's tenth novel, *Three Continents,* published in 1987, explores her favourite theme, "the almost entropic decline of generations."[37] The twins Michael and Harriet Wishwell suffer from the ills of a materialistic society. They are the children of muddled and divorced parents, a broken home seeking in vain more satisfying relationships in numerous philanderings. Both of them are dropouts but it is Michael, the brother, who first sets out in quest of an emotional sustenance. He resists the usual abodes of "hippies"—Kathmandu, Gangtok and Goa—but in Delhi and also in London he encounters the dubious Crishi, an Indian who launches an organisation of spiritual front first in America called "Fourth World Movement" which is intended to save world civilisation. His entourage consists of Rawul and Rani. Crishi becomes Michael's lover and Michael becomes a Movement devotee. Michael's sister Harriet does whatever her brother tells her to do. Thus the Wishwell millions get into the clutches of Crishi, Rawul and Rani. The scene of action shifts first to America, then to England and finally to India covering three continents. The concept of renunciation evolved by Rawul and his speeches hold his listeners under a mesmeric spell since his fourth world, he says, will be free from all present ills and limitations. Both Michael and Harriet believe in him. Harriet, the innocent rich girl, falls into the clutches of the unscrupulous fortune hunter Crishi and marries him. But Crishi is entangled in an extra-marital affair with Rani. He divides his attention and shares his bed with the two women. Rani, the legal wife of Rawul with three daughters in London, enjoys handsomely from the Wishwell estate, living and believing in opulence—a far cry from the asceticism that is associated with spiritual beings. Gradually, it is noticed that Rawul is involved in an international art smuggling ring and his Movement becomes the kingdom of *Dhoka* (the Hindi word meaning 'to trick'). Michael believes in the activities of triumvirate as the real thing but it turns out to be phoney. His naivete brings him disaster. They understand that Michael may withdraw his share of the inheritance, so Crishi orders the *Bhais* (a slang term in Hindi for men who undertake contract killings) to dispatch him. Crishi tells Harriet that Michael committed suicide. Harriet, as the narrator of the story, presents Crishi as a swine but she is madly in love with him. Her weak-willed West becomes a prey willy-nilly to such a hoax, the stronger and stouter of spirit.

Jhabvala in her eleventh novel *Poet and Dancer* (1994) reveals the nature of passion, desire, identity and the bonds of attachment which are stronger than reason, and even death. There is a deep attachment between Angel and Lara, the cousins. There is a touching contrast between them. Angel is certainly not angelic but for her unmistakable gift for poetry, and Lara is a bejewelled and vibrant dancer since her childhood. But there is deep intimacy between the two cousins. Angel and Lara are the principal protagonists of the novel. Angel's parents are Peter Koenig and Helena and Lara's parents are Dr. Hugo Manarr, a psychiatrist and Alice. Helena and Dr. Hugo are siblings. They all live in New York city. Peter's married life is disrupted as he develops an affair with a receptionist. Dr. Hugo's married life ends because his wife Alice has passed away but he keeps many girlfriends. His daughter Lara becomes neurotic and sick because she has spent a damaged childhood. She takes sleeping pills due to her tension. Angel's mother develops a relationship with an Indian business family making Angel desperate, homeless and helpless.

Dr. Hugo publishes a book on the new Psycho-evolutionary approach to the problems of psyche. Both Angel and Lara read the book. Dr. Hugo develops the method of self-perfection. Angel, a graduate, takes up a boutique business to support her mother. She becomes a vegetarian in the spirit of Dr. Hugo's book for physical purity and for the sake of her poetry. Lara is a girl with very wise and wonderful eyes. She attends acting classes. Lara's coaching is done by intuition rather than direct tuition. She accompanies her mother to India during her childhood on excursions. With her tiny cupped hands she stands before the idols and develops dancing movements. She also speaks about music. She enjoys playing the flute. But the broken domestic situations change both Angel and Lara. Angel stops writing poetry for the practical concerns in her life and Lara stops dancing involving herself in a vain love affair with Angel's father, Peter. Angel too is involved in a love affair with an Indian, Rohit, but does not dare to develop the friendship because of her attachment with Lara. Gradually, Lara becomes very weak and exhausted and feels she could do no more. Lara gets out of control and takes many pills, sleeps mysteriously. The novel ends with Angel's sitting there beside Lara in the room.

Jhabvala's twelfth novel, *Shards of Memory* (1995), like her *In Search of Love and Beauty*, traces a family through several generations, considering their long, complicated relationship with a cult-like movement. "The Master," the self-appointed spiritual leader, around whom *Shards of Memory* revolves, claims to have single-handedly ended the Second World War. Sitting in a cave in the Himalayas, he says that he invoked "high powers" through strenuous meditation. Here Jhabvala pits Western rationality against a more attractive mysticism often connected with religion which seems inexplicable to most of her European characters. Even those who do not have absolute faith in him believe in the Master and his emphatic promise to deliver "not only better world but a better Man" at least. There is Renata. She is the grand-daughter of one of the Master's most devoted followers. She gives birth to a son, Henry, at what is later calculated to be the exact moment at which the Master dies. Henry, though his parents are fair-skinned, is born dark with the Master's slanting hooded eyes and is considered by the followers to be the Master's appointed successor—quite possibly his son. On his twenty-first birthday, Henry is given a lot of money and commanded to carry on the work of the Movement. Meanwhile, Renata moves to New York. There she takes to wandering about streets, sleeping in doorways in order to prevent spiritual powers from dissolving into the vague mist in which she lives. But this brief happiness falters when she is attacked by a vagrant. Carl, her passionless lover, wants to initiate an intellectual movement in the city though there is contrast between their idealism. Thus the novel ends with the clash of idealism in this modern, cultured world.

## V

Anita Desai's writing career now spans over thirty-three years and she has so far produced ten novels and three collections of short stories. She is a very reputed and prolific Indian woman novelist of the post-Independence era. Her greatness as a contemporary novelist, according to Usha Bande, is "comparable with Iris Murdoch, Doris Lessing, Margaret Lawrence and Flora Nwapa."[38] She received the prestigious Sahitya Akademi Award for her novel, *Fire on the Mountain* in 1978, and the Federation of Indian Publisher and Authors' Guild Award for excellence in writing for *Where Shall We Go This Summer?* in 1979. Anita Desai's literary career began with her first novel, *Cry, the Peacock* (1963). Estimating the excellence of her writing, Garden comments that Anita Desai is one of the best known and highly regarded novelists working in English in the sub-continent. *Clear Light of Day* and *In Custody* (1984) were short-listed for the Booker Prize and *The Village by the Sea* (1982) won the Guardian Award for children's fiction in 1982. She is a member of the Sahitya Akademi English Board, New Delhi, and a fellow of the Royal Society of Literature in London. She has been honoured with 'Padmashri.'

Anita Desai was born in Mussoorie on 24 June 1937 of a Bengali father and a German mother. Very little is known about her life except that she was married to Ashwin Desai and has four children. Anita Desai's world, like Jane Austen's, is a restricted one. She restricts herself to writing about people and situations that she knows or can understand by deep probing. Therefore, she is known "as a pioneer in writing psychological novels or a writer of inner action."[39] Cities or places, depicted in her novels, are particularly those that have left powerful impressions on her. Calcutta impressed her so much during her short stay from 1958 to 1962 that it ultimately became a predominant character in *Voices in the City*. Similarly, Bombay and Delhi become centres of description in her other novels. Her experiences and minute observation make her novels vivacious, lively and glorious. Ila Das in *Fire on the Mountain* is a metamorphosed character. *Bye-Bye, Blackbird* is based on a visit to England when she came in touch with a large number of Indian immigrants. Desai is a novelist of cities, very good at catching the fatigue and emptiness of characters caught in melancholic existence.

Anita Desai painted her canvas with portraits of hypersensitive Maya, lonely Monisha, bored Sita, discarded Nanda Kaul, peculiar Raka, balanced Bim and simple Deven—who provide vast potential for analytical study. Anita Desai is concerned with the portrayal of psychological reality and prefers peculiar and eccentric characters to the normal ones. Scanning her art and capability of her writing, Atma Ram says that Anita Desai writes "instinctively, being carried away by her compulsions, allowing the novel to sprout and grow freely like a tree under the blue sky, and then trimming its ugly branches and uprooting weeds growing around it. The object that triggers her imagination could be very insignificant—a leaf dripping under a rain drop, a face seen on the bus, or a scrap of news read in the papers."[40] She goes to explore the inner visible section of the iceberg that one sees above the surface of the ocean "but the remaining nine-tenths of it that lie below the surface."[41]

According to Jasbir Jain, Anita Desai prefers to delve "deeper and deeper into a character or a scene, rather than going round about it."[42] She feels that a writer must have certain traits of the head and heart which are essential for writing a novel. Anita Desai is deeply concerned with the inner world of human beings and their turmoils and upheavals in their family affairs and social environment. The theme of marital dissonance and inharmonious man-woman relations figure mostly in her novels which are taken here for study. For example, Maya and Gautama in *Cry, the Peacock*, Sita and Raman in *Where Shall We Go This Summer?*, Monisha and Jiban in *Voices in the City*, Mr. and Mrs. Kaul in *Fire on the Mountain*, and Sarla and Deven in *In Custody* are locked up in unhappy wedlocks. She projects the problem of marital dissonance through incompatible couples—acutely sensitive wives, dutiful but ununderstanding and insensitive husbands. Thus her art becomes, in the words of K.R.S. Iyengar, "the exploration of sensibility—the particular kind of Indian sensibility that is ill at ease among barbarous and the philistines, the anarchists and the amoralists."[43]

Anita Desai's first novel, *Cry, the Peacock* (1963), is the sad story of the hyper-sensitive young woman Maya, married to a cold intellectual Gautama. Maya requires a love partner with wide sympathies, highly sensitive, imaginative and responsive temperaments which Gautama lacks. Maya cannot absorb herself in totality in the personality of Gautama, a mighty tree no doubt but lacking the elixir of consolation and sweetness of temperament which she may sap on. Gautama, by profession an advocate, a realistic and practical man of commonsense believing in work, guided by logic and reasoning, aims at a philosophical detachment in life visualized by the lines of the *Bhagvad Gita* reverberating through Maya's consciousness in her weak moments consoling her freakishly and yet not entering into the texture of her nature, personality and her blood veins. Therefore, conjugal bliss eludes them. Maya who is extremely distressed by a childhood prophecy of disaster, is driven to a desperate situation where her sense of reality is totally lost, leading to unseemly consequences. She kills Gautama, thinking that he does not deserve to live in the world and then she commits suicide.

The theme of marital dissonance stands out not only in *Cry, the Peacock* but also in Desai's second novel *Voices in the City* (1965). It is an unforgettable story of a Bohemian brother Nirode, and his two sisters caught in the crosscurrents of changing social values. All of them are tortured by their meaningless and hollow existence. Nirode settles down in Calcutta for a bohemian life; Monisha leads an unsuccessful married life and commits suicide. Amla is involved in an affair unsuccessfully. Temperamental incompatibility again leads to dissonance and disharmony between Monisha and Jiban. This novel presents a touching account of the unhappy, loveless life of Monisha. Like Maya, Monisha is an introvert with excessive sensitivity. Her relationship with Jiban, her husband, is marked by a total loss of communication. Jiban is financially well-off but his married life is a total failure. He treats his wife as a separate entity, as an outsider and attaches more importance to his bond with his mother. Monisha feels completely alienated from him. Her inability to bear a child, lack of intimacy with Jiban, suspicion of her in-laws in money matters and lack of privacy drive her to commit suicide. Jiban behaves like a bureaucrat with his wife. In fact, the failure of their marital life is ultimately responsible for Monisha's suicide. While Maya's husband Gautama tries at least occasionally to communicate with Maya, Jiban has neither the will nor the capability to enter and appreciate the world of Monisha.

Desai's third novel *Bye-Bye, Blackbird* (1971) deals with the psychic turmoil of Sarah an English girl, who is married to an Indian boy, Adit. She comes to India and struggles to find her identity since she is alienated both socially and psychologically. Adit, Dev and Sarah suffer deeply from existentialist problems.

The optimistic and mysterious environment of London fascinates Dev, but for Adit it creates disgust and homesickness which make him leave England. In this novel, Desai seeks to explore East-West encounter. Sarah is fixed between East and West for philosophical and sociological needs, but the more urgent need to define her own identity leads to familial disharmony. The novel explores the love-hate relationship of the immigrants with the society of their adoption. It reveals the impossibility of total assimilation in another culture. Desai ends the novel without any solution to the highly complex "double net" of the immigrant experience.

The fourth novel, *Where Shall We Go This Summer?*, again deals with the theme of marital dissonance emanating from the conflict between two irreconcilable temperaments and two diametrically-opposed viewpoints. Sita, the central character in the novel, is a nervous, sensitive middle-aged woman. Like Maya and Gautama in *Cry, the Peacock*, the relationship between Sita and Raman in this novel is disrupted because of their inability to understand each other. Sita is alienated from Raman and their children because of her emotionally melodramatic reactions to small incidents and things. Her marriage with Raman, an industrialist based in Bombay, is not successful in any sense in spite of children and financial security. As a child she happened to live a life close to nature on an island where her father wielded great power through his supposed magic spell on its populace. The incompatibility of the down-to-earth life of Bombay and Sita's repressed childhood wishes fixing on her father play havoc with her sensitivity. During her fifth pregnancy, an unconscious urge leads her to the island where she seeks to keep the child unborn which is an indication of an unrealistic solution to her problems. At the end of the novel, she realises that the bonds which are developed around her cannot be broken easily. Therefore, she compromises with life in mastering the present in terms of the past. Thus Raman proves to be better than Gautama and

Jiban since he attempts to understand and adjust and wins Sita back.

*Fire on the Mountain* (1977), Desai's fifth novel, deals with the protagonist Mrs. Nanda Kaul's determined detachment, non-involvement and unhappy conjugal ties throughout her life. She leads a life of deprivation of unfulfilment in a house of a Vice-Chancellor, Mr. Kaul, apparently teeming with plenty except true love. In order to illustrate this, the novelist explores the inner emotional world of Mrs. Nanda Kaul who has had too much of the world with her and so longs for a quiet, retired life at Carignano in Kasauli because she had a meaningless marital life with her husband who maintained an extra-marital affair with a Lecturer. At the new hill station she is free from demands. Her great-granddaughter Raka joins her. Raka's stunning capability to change things makes Mrs. Nanda Kaul discover new needs within herself. When violence breaks out due to the death of Ila Das, who was raped, Mrs. Nanda Kaul dies of shock.

The presence of another woman in Mr. Kaul's life creates in Mrs. Nanda Kaul such a sickness of soul that she distrusts all attachments and affairs. In Anita Desai's earlier novels *Cry, the Peacock, Voices in the City* and *Where Shall We Go This Summer?*, the incompatibility of temperaments or psychic complexes cause marital dissonance but it is an extra-marital affair that disturbs the marital equation in *Fire on the Mountain.*

Desai focuses on the theme of forgiveness in her sixth novel, *Clear Light of Day* (1980). Bim, the chief female protagonist, after a long period of frustration and alienation with her younger brother Raja comes to realise the importance of relationships and the need to forget and forgive. Bim, after the death of his parents, wants Raja to be in the house with siblings but he goes to Hyderabad at the instance of Hyder Ali, the landlord of the house in Old Delhi. Bim's other sister, Tara, marries Bakul and lives independently. Raja marries Hyder Ali's daughter Benazir and becomes the landlord of Bim's house. He hurts Bim's feelings by writing a letter stating that she can continue to stay in the house with the same rent. Bim gets alienated with this letter and wants to keep herself away from Raja forever. She does not like to run away leaving her mentally handicapped brother, Baba. She discards all modes of escape. Desai's Nanda Kaul escapes to Carignano mountain, Sita goes to Manori island, but Bim does not go anywhere. She sees all these changes in the clear light of day; she is definitely disturbed but also realises the importance of an attitude to forget and forgive by re-unifying herself with Raja.

Anita Desai's seventh novel, *The Village by the Sea* (1983), is totally free from the seminal and familial pre-occupations of adult human psyche. She probes the labyrinthine lanes of teen-ager consciousness in this novel. The theme of the novel is the tragic predicament of Hari, resident of Thul village situated on the Western coast of India. The problem here is one of survival in a society at cross-roads between tradition and transition, the rural way and the urban scientific and sophisticated approach to life. The novel is about the children but the problem centres round the issues of eternal importance to the adult world. Hari is the son of a fisherman. His parents and siblings depend upon his earnings. The new proposals to establish factories in the village disturbing the traditional professions give a jolt to Hari. At this critical juncture, Sayiid Ali, an ornithologist, exhorts Hari to adapt and accommodate himself just like the birds. Desai voices this survival motif through the bird-watcher which is the reverse of existential alienation. The emotional psyche of mal-adjustment does not find any place in this novel. Therefore, as the birds move from place to place to adapt new methods for survival, Hari goes to Bombay, suffers for some period, learns watch-repairing and yearns for homecoming. Thus the message "The Wheel Turns" speaks of the theme of the novel.

Marital dissonance in Desai's eighth novel *In Custody* (1984) is not so much psychological and philosophical as economic. Deven is a temporary lecturer in Hindi at a local college in Mirpore. Bitterness sets in the relationship with his wife Sarla whose materialistic ambitions remain unfulfilled. His world of reality is characterized by tensions resulting from financial problems. He is caught between his dissatisfied wife and the obligation of his job which he finds difficult to face due to lack of confidence. To escape from this real world, he courts a world of fantasy which consists of hopes of confirmation and promotion in college, fame through successful accomplishment of his literary projects, cultivation of his love for Urdu poetry and procurement of money, but the harsh reality forces him out of the world of fantasy. His attempt to escape from the world of fantasy results in total disaster. Ultimately, he is forced to compromise with the dull and mundane reality of life. Desai deals with the theme of death in her ninth novel *Baumgartner's Bombay* (1988). She presents history from Nazi Germany to contemporary India and a complicated sociology through the experiences of the lovable but clumsy old Hugo Baumgartner, the protagonist of the novel. He is a German migrant in India without any kith or kin. He is humane towards all those who come in contact with him. To solve the financial problem of a drug-addict Kurt, Baumgartner takes him to his house out of his fellow-feeling and compassion. But Kurt stabs Baumgartner brutally for the sake of silver trophies. Desai thus points out man's inhumanity to man. This is a sad commentary on the life of urbanites who are the victims of social evils in the form of drug-addiction and unemployment.

Desai's tenth novel *Journey to Ithaca* (1995) touches upon the sensitive theme of spiritual quest. Its title is taken from Constantine Cavafy's (a Greek poet, 1863-1933) poem 'Ithaca'—a metaphor for Utopia. The two protagonists of the novel are from the hippie generation that thronged India in the 60s. It is the story of Matteo, an Italian young man, who abandons his studies and secures elite life to come to India to search for spiritual enlightenment in the *ashrams* of India. His journalist wife, the practical and down-to-earth Sophie, accompanies him but does not find the mysterious Mother of Pondicherry as inspiring a *guru* as he regards her. As Matteo worships at the Mother's feet, Sophie struggles for his love. After they encounter different stages of being stranded in a spiritual wasteland, their hostility to each other vitiates the quest. Desai concludes the novel by stating that the West looked to India as a spiritual land during the period of Annie Besant, Sri Aurobindo and Ruth St. Denis, but now it is spiritually a wasteland.

VI

The novels of Jhabvala have portrayed modern India to an ever-growing number of English readers all over the world. In the first comprehensive study of her work, Yasmine Gooneratne, a critic and a woman of letters of much distinction, examines both the impact upon Jhabvala's writing of the complex Indian experience and its result; the steady development to her present maturity of one of the finest contemporary fiction writers and ironists. Gooneratne argues very convincingly that in Jhabvala's fiction "the theme of loneliness and isolation," besides the theme of "sensibility of the Western expatriate in India is almost pervasive."[44] Another critic of Jhabvala, V.A. Shahane, in his full-length critical appraisal of her work, assesses her literary art, her use of irony, depth of feeling and fictional craft. He highlights her talents and examines her constant concern with India, and the variegated patterns of life. As an Indian English woman writer, she brings to the literary scene a skilfully-drawn picture of life as she has experienced it. Shahane finds in his study "the interaction between two cultures, the European and the Indian. In fact, "it is her *forte* since it is in this area that her personal experience in India is transformed into art."[45] A noted scholar and critic of Jhabvala, H.M. Williams, probes the concept of traditional Hinduism which "has recognised the validity of life of the householder, husband, father and bread-winner, as long as this is limited to a phase of a man's life, giving to the spiritual as he grows older."[46] It is Ramlal Agarwal who emphatically argued, for the first time, that in Jhabvala's fiction "Indian spirituality is an escape from Indian poverty. Jhabvala has said time and again that

India demoralises Europeans who come out to stay here. This is also a major theme in her novels."[47] Different critical reviews and critical studies of Jhabvala's works have been published in several volumes. Laurie Sucher, for instance, states that Jhabvala's "fiction usually centres on the lives of women which leads her to observe the issues that feminism grapples with; how women get, use and maintain power in a society that renders them effectively powerless."[48]

The question of women's empowerment is crucial to the novels of Anita Desai too. But in Desai's novels, it is the power of the female/feminine psyche that renders her characters almost neurotic. It could be argued that the novels of Anita Desai have an existential and psychological bearing. She projects the difficulties faced by her characters in shedding their fears and insecurities, which results in an unauthentic existence making them anxious and full of despair. Her novels depict the workings of unseen forces on the human mind and psyche. A close reading of her fiction reveals that she portrays with amazing accuracy the inward odyssey and psychic upheavals of hypersensitive people struggling to survive in difficult human situations. Mrinalini Solanki opines that the general problem in the novels of Desai is of "self-consciousness of characters and the recurring theme is self-awareness and self-identity."[49] There is intense questioning and the protagonists are torn between their search for authentic existence and the limitations of the human situations that prevent them from such realisations. Kunj Bala Goel's study focuses on Anita Desai's verbal patterns in relation to her thematic rhythms. It is a useful work in order to understand the relationship between linguistic and literary studies in general. Goel points out that the major theme in Desai's fiction is unattainable withdrawal. "Sometimes instead of fighting they [the protagonists] tend only to withdraw; but to their shock, in time, they realise that their attempts are futile because withdrawal is unattainable."[50] Usha Bande, an eminent critic of Desai's fiction, explores the concept of "*Karma* theory running through entire narrative of *Cry, the Peacock* and the depiction of woman's plight in modern Indian society in Desai's novels confirms the fact that modern Indian woman's psychic turmoil reveals an era of awakening."[51] Another critic, Bidulata Choudhury, observes that the theme of "the emancipation of women and necessary steps to be taken for it, is found on page after page in her novels."[52] In a very suggestive way, the critic Usha Pathania discovers that "the protagonists desire and strive for a more authentic way of life than the one offered to them."[53]

The present study which is concerned with the theme of marital dissonance in the novels of Jhabvala and Desai will examine the extent to which both these authors, despite their divergent attitudes, perceive this problem creatively. In fact, a comparative analysis of the works of Jhabvala and Desai in their treatment of man-woman relationship would be quite stimulating and interesting. This would help one to discover a pattern of human relationships emerging under the weight of multi-dimensional pressures and tensions. While Anita Desai dwells on the predicament and dilemma faced by the urban middle-class who are pre-occupied with the hard realities of workaday life, Jhabvala explores the feminine predicament in the socio-economic situations and their impact on life at personal and domestic levels faced by the urban middle-class in Delhi. The prime concern of Anita Desai has been the exploration of the inner selves of her women protagonists. They vividly exemplify the dilemma stemming from the contemporary chaos created by crumbling values. While Anita Desai explores and portrays kinship bonds from the viewpoint of a psychologist, Jhabvala focuses on the impact of diverse socio-economic problems upon the even flow of primary ties.

## NOTES

1. Virginia Woolf, *Contemporary Writers* (London: Hogarth, 1965) p. 26.

2. C Vimala Rao, "Women and Fiction," *The Literary Half-Yearly*, Vol. VII, No. 1 (Winter 1966), p. 47.
3. David Krech, et al., *Individual in Society* (University California: Berkley, McGraw Hill Book Company, 1962), p. 480.
4. *Ibid.*, p. 214.
5. *Ibid.*, p. 383.
6. A.K. Sur, *Sex and Marriage in India: An Ethno-Historical Survey* (Bombay: Allied, 1973), p. 2.
7. Alexander Walker, *Woman; Physiologically Considered as to Mind, Morals, Marriage, Matrimonial Slavery, Infidelity and Divorce* (Delhi: Mittal, 1987), p. 78.
8. S. Pothen, *Divorce: Its Causes and Consequences in Hindu Society* (New Delhi: Shakti Press, 1987), p. 2.
9. Charles Cooley, *Social Consciousness,* p. 368 qtd. Pandarinath H. Prabhu, *Hindu Social Organisation: A Study in Socio-Psychological and Ideological Foundations* (Bombay: Popular, 1958), p. 238.
10. Subhash Chandra, "Family and Marriage" in Shobha De's *Socialite Evenings*," *Indian Women Novelists,* set I, vol. 1, ed. R.K. Dhawan (New Delhi: Prestige, 1991), p. 244.
11. D.H. Lawrence, "Morality and the Novel," *20th Century Literature Criticism*, ed. David Lodge (London: Longman, 1972), p. 130.
12. A.V. Krishna Rao, "The Novels of Kamala Markandaya: A Study," *Studies in Contemporary Indian Fiction in English*, ed. A.N. Dwivedi (Allahabad: Kitab Mahal, 1987), p. 113.
13. *Ibid.*, p. 220.
14. R.S. Singh, *Indian Novel in English* (Delhi: Arnold-Heinemann, 1977), p. 142.
15. Nayanatara Sahgal, "Woman, Persons or Possessions," *The Hindustan Times*, (Sunday), July 19, 1970.
16. *Ibid.*
17. Sarabjit Sandhu, "The Image of Woman in *That Long Silence*" in *Indian Women Novelists*, set I, vol. 5, ed. R.K. Dhawan, p. 138.
18. M. Sivaramakrishna, "Bharati Mukherjee," *Indian English Novelists: An Anthology of Critical Essays*, ed. Madhusudhan Prasad (New Delhi: Sterling, 1982), p. 73.

19. Jasbir Jain, "Foreignness of Spirit: The World of Bharati Mukherjee's Novels," *The Journal of Indian Writing in English*, vol. XIII, no. 2 (1985), p. 17.
20. R.P. Jhabvala, "Moonlight, Jasmine and Rickets," *New York Times*, 23 April 1973, p. 35.
21. John Updike, "Raman and Daisy and Olivia and the Nawab," review of *Heat and Dust* in *The New Yorker*, 5 July 1978, p. 83.
22. Ramlal Agarwal,"Outsider with Unusual Insight," *The Times of India* (Bombay), 25 March 1973, p. 11.
23. Laurie Sucher, *The Fiction of R..P. Jhabvala: The Politics of Passion* (London: Macmillan, 989), pp. 4-5.
24. Ramlal Agarwal, *R.P. Jhabvala: A Study of Her Fiction* (New Delhi: Sterling, 1990), p. 112.
25. Yasmine Gooneratne, *Silence, Exile and Cunning* (New Delhi; Orient Longman, 1983), p. 18.
26. H.M. Williams, *The Fiction of Ruth Prawer Jhabvala* (Calcutta: Writers' Workshop, 1973), p. 12.
27. Linda Warley, "The Cuckoo's Nest: House and Home in Two Early Novels by Ruth Prawer Jhabvala," *Passages to Ruth Prawer Jhabvala*, ed. Ralph J. Crane (New Delhi: Sterling, 1991), p. 22.
28. H.M. Williams, p. 33.
29. *Ibid.*, p. 10.
30. *Ibid.*, p. 49.
31. R.P. Jhabvala, *A New Dominion* (London: John Murray, 1972), p. 26.
32. *Ibid.*, p. 2.
33. V.A. Shahane, "Ruth Prawer Jhabvala's *New Dominion,"* *Journal of Commonwealth Literature*, vol. 12, No. 1 (August 1977), p. 48.
34. Hariprasanna, "Expatriate Woman in Jhabvala's Fiction," in *Indian Women Novelists* ed. R.K. Dhawan, set III, Vol. 3 (New Delhi: Prestige, 1995), p. 23.
35. Laurie Sucher, *The Fiction of Ruth Prawer Jhabvala*, p. 168.
36. S.R. Jalote, "Ruth Jhabvala's *In Search of Love and Beauty*: A Study in Quest and Disillusion," in *Indian Women-Novelists* ed. R.K. Dhawan, set III, Vol. 3 (New Delhi: Prestige, 1995), p. 34.
37. Laurie Sucher, p. 206.

38. Usha Bande, *The Novels of Anita Desai* (The cover page) (New Delhi: Prestige Books, 1988).
39. Bidulata Choudhury, *Women and Society in the Novels of Anita Desai* (New Delhi: Creative, 1995), p. 45.
40. Atma Ram, "An Interview with Anita Desai," *World Literature Written in English*, vol. 15, No. 1 (April 1977), p. 100.
41. Anita Desai replies to the "Questionnaire," *Kakatiya Journal of English Studies*, Vol. III, No. 1 (1978), p. 1.
42. Jasbir Jain, "An Interview with Anita Desai," *Stairs to the Attic: The Novels of Anita Desai* (Jaipur: Printwell, 1987), p. 14.
43. K.R.S. Iyengar, *Indian Writing in English* (New Delhi: Sterling, 1983), p. 464.
44. Yasmine Gooneratne, p. 2.
45. V.A. Shahane, *Ruth Prawer Jhabvala* (Calcutta: Writers' Workshop, 1983), p. 20.
46. H.M. Williams, *The Fiction of Ruth Prawer Jhabvala*, p. 12.
47. Ramlal Agarwal, *Ruth Prawer Jhabvala*), pp. 7-8.
48. Laurie Sucher, p. 6.
49. Mrinalini Solanki, *Anita Desai's Fiction: Patterns of Survival Strategies* (Delhi: Kanishka, 1992), p. 2.
50. Kunj Bala Goel, *Language and Theme in Anita Desai's Fiction* (Jaipur: Classic, 1989), p. 21.
51. Usha Bande, p. 13.
52. Bidulata Choudhury, p. 47.
53. Usha Pathania, *Human Bonds and Bondages: The Fiction of Anita Desai and Kamala Markandaya* (Delhi: Kanishka, 1992), p. 12.

Chapter II

# A Study of Ruth Prawer Jhabvala's Novels

No survey of contemporary Indian literary scene would be complete if it failed to take note of the writings of Ruth Prawer Jhabvala. She is one of the most outstanding Indian novelists in English. She is Polish-German by birth, English by education and Indian by marriage. Her novels stand in a unique relationship to Indian literature in English. Khushwant Singh, while bracketing Ruth Prawer Jhabvala with R.K. Narayan, calls her "a fine interpreter of contemporary India in fiction."[1] Perhaps this remark, seen in the light of Jhabvala's achievement as a literary artist, is of course true. As a writer writing about India, she has earned a coveted place among the novelists of contemporary India. She has acquired a rare grasp of the Indian situation by virtue of the special status of her marriage to an Indian and her stay in India. Her deep interest and involvement with the life around her has provided her with an angle of vision sufficiently distinct from those of Westerners who wrote about India. Thoroughly familiar with life and manners of her adopted country, she has been at the same time, gifted with the Western sensibility which endows her with a unique insight into the typical traits of Indians, particularly the structure of lives of urban upper and lower middle classes as they keep on undulating between tradition and modernity. She, therefore, presents with utmost care and sympathy the Indian tradition, culture, civilization, manners, systems, pattern of living and values. The major issues that form the theme of marital dissonance in five of her novels taken up for study here are rooted in the clash between orthodox tradition of a male-dominated Indian society and modernity, between materialism and genuine idealism and finally the East-West encounter.

Jhabvala's two novels, viz. *The Householder* (1960) and *Get Ready for Battle* (1962), offer Indian domestic setting engulfed with the dichotomy between traditionalism and modernism, between materialism and idealism and also the clash of general attitudes and personalities. In her novels *Esmond in India* (1958) and *A Backward Place* (1965), she also deals with the theme of marital dissonance in the light of divergences between the Eastern and the Western cultural values and their encounter. In her famous novel, *Heat and Dust* (1975), Jhabvala traces the reasons of marital dissonance in the clash between the pragmatist approach and the dreamy approach; and the dissonance is attributed to the emotional dissatisfaction associated with psychological depression of the wife because of the husband's pre-occupation with his profession.

The Indian problems and conflicts with reference to marital dissonance are dealt by both Indian English and Anglo-Indian writers. The Indian English writers peeped into the cause of marital dissonance with the help of sentimentalism and mysticism. The Anglo-Indian writers probed the situation and pronounced the judgements without really attempting to understand the prevailing conditions of Indian society. But Jhabvala, in her novels, does not take either of these two extreme stances of judgements. She writes about the furious social scuffling of the present-day Indians revealing the tragedy beneath the social evils. As a novelist, she is mainly concerned with the personal and domestic set-up of large united or joint families focussing the differences of young married couples either within or with the problems of adjustment of expatriates against the Indian background and with the problems of couples separated from their husbands. Appreciating the artistic talent of Jhabvala, Haydn Moore Williams rightly remarks: "perhaps in the technical sense, she [Jhabvala] is the best fiction writer now writing in India about India."[2]

## 1 The Indian Ethos, Domesticity and Society: *The Householder* and *Get Ready for Battle*

Jhabvala knows that in the Indian ethos there is a struggle between two principles—the inescapable sense of the past and the new compulsive urge for modernity. This type of struggle is seen nowhere better than in the Indian family system which is facing a quick re-organisation under the influence of economic and social changes. Until recently, the joint family system[3] was the prevailing pattern in the family organisation of India. Now there is a sudden change in the set-up of family organisation with the independent style of life due to growing industrialisation. Jhabvala, as the novelist of social behaviour, finds the joint family system as a source of misery. She exemplified this in her novel, *The Householder*[4] where the protagonist, Prem, who was under the influence of traditional family structure, suffers a lot in his conjugal relationship; but later the sense of modernisation lifts his feelings of reciprocity for a better and happy life with total understanding and reconciliation.

The title of Jhabvala's novel, *The Householder*, provides its own frame of reference. The dominant Hindu view of life, which took shape during the ten centuries that are generally believed to have elapsed between the composition of the Upanishads and the formulation of the codes of Manu and Kautilya (roughly 500 B.C. to A.D. 500), classifies the life of the 'householder' as the second of four *Ashrams* or stages in Aryan life. Preceded by the period of studentship, it is followed by retirement and calm reflection, and finally by the renunciation of all worldly interests.[5]

In the novel, *The Householder*, Prem is the protagonist. Prem's father provides an extreme instance of the traditional *pater-familias*. He was a strict disciplinarian committed to the orthodox way of life. He was a seemingly remote, aloof and much-feared figure in the family. Prem and his sisters never felt at ease with their father. He was a total dictator. Prem's mother was submissive and oppressive to his father. All the members of the family tried their level best to change the attitude of the head of the family. He was such a dictator that in the house everybody tried to keep him happy with due reverence to his status. This applied to his food habits also: "In the house everybody had had to tiptoe past his study, and at meal-times he always had some special dish cooked, in which no one else had been allowed to share" (28). Prem, who was married at a young age, unfortunately adopted his father's attitude in his marital relationship. Jhabvala provides the direct impressions of Prem's life who suffers from familial, financial and professional problems besides the aggressive temperament of his wife, Indu. In fact, Prem's character can be compared with Gulzari Lal of *Get Ready for Battle* as both have the same bent of mind. In contrast, Prem's wife, Indu is a modernist. She wants luxury and comfort. She fights with her husband for pleasures, freedom within the house, and she always supports the commands of her mother. Whereas in *Get Ready for Battle*, Gulzari Lal's wife, Sarla Devi, is slightly different. Sarla Devi is an idealist; she fights with her husband not for herself but for others [slum-dwellers].

However, the circle of the Householder is quite limited. Prem is a Hindi lecturer in Mr. Khanna's private college in Delhi. He is from a lower middle class milieu. He draws a meagre sum of Rs. 175 a month. Of these he pays Rs. 45 towards rent. He pays for a maidservant in order to maintain his social status as a lecturer in a college. Consequently, he is in a severe financial crisis. His employer and his landlord are obviously exploiting his abilities and necessities. Besides all these things, he is an unsuccessful lecturer in the class. His classroom discipline is more or less in a mess. His students do not respect him whereas his colleague Mr. Chaddha, Professor of History, receives wonderful response and respect from the students both in the classroom and outside. Prem suffers a lot from an inferiority complex because of his inability to control the students in the classroom.

Prem is very close to Mr. Sohan Lal, Professor of Mathematics. He exchanges ideas, opinions, views and professional feelings with Sohan Lal. But Sohan Lal too, has his own financial problems. Prem sympathises with him. He wants to speak to Mr. Khanna for a raise in Sohan Lal's salary with an intention to give an indirect hint for a raise in his own salary. He is worried because his wife Indu is pregnant; and he feels that with a baby at home, the domestic expenses would go up. He meets and tells Principal Khanna:

> How can he [Sohan Lal] support so many people on Rs. 175=00 per month? He took another step forward and said in a voice passionate with conviction and pity, poverty and want are terrible things. In the *Panchatantra*, it is written, 'It is better to be dead than Poor.' Mr. Khanna said, 'It is an interesting thought.' (12)

Prem plans throughout the novel to ask for a raise in salary, but he never succeeds in his attempts.

Another aspect of his financial problem which haunts him is the house rent. The salary is 175 rupees. "How to manage on that? His rent alone came to 45 rupees" (8). Prem tries himself, and he tries through his wife to approach the Seigals, their landlords, for a reduction of the rent. At one stage, the old woman, Prem's mother, during her short sojourn at her son is asked to try for the reduction of the rent. The only result of his approach is that he gets a cold reply from the landlords. Added to these, Prem also has problems related to marital dissonance. While "Prem strives to establish himself in the linked roles of husband, bread-winner and householder, Indu finds some difficulty in accommodating her individual, lively outlook to the requirements of her role as married woman and housewife."[6] She comes from a fun-loving family. She wishes to be a credit to her parents and to Prem but she cannot help being amused by the very idea of herself as the dignified lady of the 'household.'

In the beginning, the relationship between Prem and Indu is rather formal and impersonal. Trained in the traditional way, Prem has learnt from elders that a wife should be subservient to her husband; and he expects from his wife unquestioning obedience. The actual quarrel between Prem and Indu takes place when they receive letters from their respective mothers. Referring to her mother's letter, Indu says in a low voice:

> 'She [Indu's mother] wants me to come home.' Prem had no comments to make. It did not, he thought, greatly matter to him whether she stayed or went.
>
> Indu confessed, 'I wrote to her about . . .' and 'Yes, Yes,' said Prem in some irritation. 'That is why she wants me to come home,' Indu said.
>
> 'My mother is coming to visit us,' Prem said. After thinking this over for a while, Indu said, 'Then she will be able to look after you here when I am gone.'
>
> 'How can you go away when my mother is coming to visit us?' 'Why not?' Indu inquired. The innocence of her voice as she asked this made him quite angry. He shouted, 'What do you mean why not? Have you no sense?' She looked at him with her eyes wide in amazement. He had never before shouted at her.
>
> Now that he had started, he rather felt like shouting some more. But he thought of the Seigals downstairs and the servant-boy in the kitchen and so changed to a fierce whisper. 'Don't you understand that my mother will be offended?' he hissed, supporting himself on one elbow as he lay on the bed and leaning towards her.
>
> 'Why are you whispering?' she asked.
>
> 'How stupid you are—do you want everyone to hear us quarrelling?'
>
> 'I am not quarrelling.'
>
> He lay back again, feeling rather defeated. How stupid she is, he thought; one could not even argue with her.
>
> Indu said, 'My mother wants me to come home.'
>
> 'But how can you, when my mother is coming?' He tried to sound terribly reasonable but only succeeded in sounding annoyed.
>
> 'All girls go home when they are . . .'
>
> 'Not at the beginning. Only in the end, when their time has come.'
>
> 'Yes, at the beginning also.' (22-23)

The conversation shatters whatever mental tranquillity he had possessed before the hot discussion:

> He felt sorry for himself, to be married to a wife who was not only quite different from what he had wished and hoped for, but who also opposed in his wishes. (24)

Prem wondered whether other people's wives behaved like this too. He longed to talk to someone about his married life. It was such a new and unknown thing for him. It was a serious tension to his mind. "He began to feel like crying himself; already a tear was trembling on his cheek. He brushed it aside with his hand and the feel of it made him want to cry more. He felt so alone and lonely, shut up in this small ugly flat with Indu who cried by herself in the sitting-room while he had to lie and cry by himself in the bedroom." (24)

Though Prem gets bored in his congested flat because of the indifferent attitude of his wife, he does not allow his routine schedule to attend college and to attend to domestic needs to get disturbed. However, he tends to spend most of his time among his friends. He gets home sometimes late in the night. He feels that his wife should not sleep though it is too late but should serve him food and sleep then. One day, he gets home late and finds Indu lying on the bed fast asleep. He was hungry and angry. Then he feels: "it was not right for a wife to go to sleep before she had served her husband however late he had come." (46)

The next morning, he leaves for college. He gets back home for lunch. He finds his wife in an angry mood. He finds it difficult to establish good relationship with his wife. Indu also is not happy with Prem. She wants to go to her mother's place at the earliest. Prem's mother has already come to them. Therefore, she plans to go. She packs her suitcase but Prem refuses permission. His standard answer is; 'I have forbidden' (50). But Prem's wife being bold and individualistic declares her independence, retorting, 'Who are you to forbid?' (50)

While Prem is already worried about marital dissonance, his mother compounds the problems between Prem and Indu. Her uninvited arrival in Prem's house widens the chasm of insecurity between them. Her presence means that "the atmosphere in their small flat became rather strained' (63). Now, Indu and Prem can no longer move freely in their own house. Besides this, Prem's mother creates a sense of frustration and irritation in Indu by passing comments on Indu. Indu takes to going to bed early as a way of avoiding her mother-in-law's critical comments and glances. The maladjustment in the context of Indian family system between daughter-in-law and mother-in-law is portrayed by Jhabvala very effectively in the novel. The mother-in-law throws accusations at the daughter-in-law who bears them in silent hostility or at the most, obliquely expressing her wrath on others. As a result of these unfavourable situations, Indu suddenly goes to her mother with her uncle in her husband's absence, leaving no message. Prem, like a typical husband, feels insulted at Indu's leaving the house like that.

The turning point in their life comes when Prem's friend Sohan Lal takes him to the Swami where his songs made Prem's head and heart light; and he laughed. The Swami suggests to Prem to get adjusted in the real life first before taking a decision to join in the spiritual life. Jhabvala observes:

> All his [Prem's] former worries about his rent, his rise in salary, his lack of authority as a teacher and husband were nothing but a thin scum floating on top of a deep well of happiness and satisfaction. Nothing, he thought, would ever trouble him again. From now on he would live in contemplation only of spiritual things. (57)

Indu's absence makes Prem realise how much he values her presence. He cannot talk about how he feels about her, he makes gestures that signify his love. He buys for her a glittering and beautiful blouse-piece, and writes a letter wherein he expresses his passion for her:

> The house is empty without you and my heart also is empty. . . . I want to stroke you and kiss you everywhere with my mouth and then I want to be inside you. When I think of this I feel I shall die with longing so much for you. (103)

Now, he realises that the reconciliation for a happy adjustment in married life is only through mutual affection. He finds in such a relationship not only affection but sympathy, love and psychological security. Moreover, through his experience, he understands that the profound conjugal relationship and affection for each other is generated in husband and wife not merely by physical contact but also by working together in the family and by sharing other's joys and sorrows. This awareness of a growing sense of love and affection towards his wife makes Prem take a decision to send his mother away from him to Bangalore where his sister lives. The moment his mother boards the train for Bangalore, he hurries home to Indu. On the night of his mother's departure, Prem and Indu sleep on the roof of their apartment building. "The couple's wish to sleep outside is indicative of their new relationship."[7] Now, they are at ease with each other. Now they are not alone as alienated individuals anymore; now they are in a relationship which can be ideally described as one where individuals can experience feelings of complete union with each other. With these changes in their feelings, Indu becomes Prem's main source of consolation. He feels he has achieved something as a husband. Now, his status in the college does not matter very much. Prem is matured enough to find happiness in what he has and in his confidence in his role of a householder.

As a token of their last cherished desire to invite Raj [Prem's old friend] and his wife for dinner to have good social image, they invite them and, in return, Raj compliments Indu for her delicious cooking: "it seems your wife is a very good cook" (139). With this compliment both Indu and Prem feel a sense of achievement. This achievement is a result of a common decision and combined action of Prem and Indu. They realise that freedom and equality are the bases of personal happiness in a family. Prem, throwing away and brushing aside the established concept of traditional style of life which has created a gulf between the wife and husband, now submits himself to the cause of better conjugal life to which his wife responds positively and happily. Indu too feels that now she is the queen of the house. Thus, the novel ends with the feeling that Prem and Indu are finally at home.

While *The Householder* begins with marital dissonance and ends with consummation of marital love, *Get Ready for Battle* (1962)[8] goes beyond, and portrays the new problems confronting the modern family and the consequent dissonance in the husband-wife relationship. Gulzari Lal and Sarla Devi, though married for many years, have discordance in their married life. The clash of attitudes appears to be the cause of the dissonance. Gulzari Lal with the scum of traditional ways with the modern views is a strong believer in genuine idealism. Sarla, the heroine of the novel, has an interesting background. She was born into a Kshatriya family of Punjab of the pre-partition India. For ages, it has been the tradition of Kshatriyas that the women were not permitted to move out except for performing religious ceremonies and for dispensing charity. But Sarla Devi is against such conditions laid for women. She represents the modern woman with powerful and strong ideals to be fulfilled, irrespective of the consequences. Her marriage with Gulzari Lal is not the traditionally arranged one. She agreed to marry him for the spirit he showed in choosing her as his wife. But she insists on maintaining her freedom after the marriage. Gulzari Lal too consents but quickly switches over to traditional rules of Kshatriyas ignoring his promise. Thus they begin their married life with clashes. The concept of a wife according to Gulzari Lal is traditional. She should give him companionship and solace after his day's work, entertaining him with lively talk, engaging herself with the duties of a wife with no interest outside the house. Basically, he was attracted by Sarla Devi's beautiful figure and impulsive nature and took the decision to marry her.

It is believed that Indian life is motivated by idealistic aspects of life. Preoccupation with the life beyond and contemplative habit of mind, the purposive mode of discharging one's duty without concern for its fruits, the spirit of renunciation are considered as the fundamental precepts of Indian idealism which is strongly linked with and influenced by Indian spiritualism. Here, Sarla Devi represents such an idealistic bent of mind, life and practice. Gulzari Lal, her husband, though traditional in his thinking in controlling his wife, is modern and purely materialistic in his practical life.

Strictly speaking, materialism in India cannot be said to be an outcome of scientific and industrial progress. In fact, it has been in vogue since the time of Charvaka,[9] the founder of Indian materialism. According to him, materialism stands for sensualism, self-gratification and individual assertion conforming itself to material happiness. It advocates the doctrine of pleasure and enjoyment. "Eat, drink and be merry, death comes to all closing our lives"[10] is the slogan of this materialistic school of thought. Such a hedonistic view of life is very much prevalent even in the present day. V.A. Shahane observes: "Jhabvala, like George Bernard Shaw and E.M. Forster, is deeply conscious of the value of money in modern life and the fact that all idealistic schemes of restructuring civilization will need money for their implementation in practical life."[11]

Jhabvala traces these materialistic tendencies through the character of Gulzari Lal in her novel *Get Ready for Battle* which depicts extreme materialism of rich, corrupt, bourgeoisie of contemporary India. In the novel, the novelist deals with a number of intrigues—sexual, familial, social and also with the theme of marital dissonance in the upper middle class, money-minded urban society. All the characters in the novel are connected with the broken and disintegrated marriage of the Delhi-based Punjabi businessman, Mr. Gulzari Lal. The sense of misunderstanding, incompatibility, the clash of attitudes in terms of materialism and idealism and the mismatched feelings take a serious turn in the novel. Gulzari Lal is a brash businessman who throws big parties to dazzle petty Government officials:

> no one was bored, for almost everybody in the room could be of use to someone else and this was stimulating. There was a Commissioner who was stimulating to a number of fairly high-ranking

> civil servants, who were in their turn stimulating to a number of middle-ranking civil servants and so on, down to the municipal engineer for whom the party was made by the presence of the Vice-Chairman of his Board. An overall stimulus was provided by a Maharaja, an imposing figure who, now that his kingdom and good deal of his income were gone, was taking an interest in business affairs; he was really of no importance to anyone, but his presence made everyone feel they had got into good company and had come a long way from where they had started. (7)

In contrast, Sarla Devi strongly believes in austerity and high moral principles. She wants to act according to her conscience. That is the reason she had "hundreds of interests away from him [Gulzari Lal], her swamis and politicians, her refusal ever to be a wife such as he wanted and thought he had a right to expect" (38). Therefore, these differences which are linked with materialism and idealism wreck their marriage. She abandons the world of pleasure for being socially useful. She is more worried about the miserable life of the poor people of Bundi Busti (Slum locality) in Delhi than the needs of her husband. She regards her separation from her husband and her family as a form of self-indulgence as she wants to work more for the people of Bundi Basti. Jhabvala observes: "all through their married life, whenever he had wanted her, she had been busy with something else; she had many interests and none of them had ever included him" (35). Thus the married life of the Lals is completely disrupted and disintegrated.

'When the clashes become intense, Sarla Devi walks out of the house and settles in her brother, Mr. Brij Mohan's house. She devotes all the time for the poor people of Bundi Busti. The temperaments and ideologies of the husband and wife are not at all conducive to adjustments. Since Gulzari Lal needs a wife to attend on him personally, he takes a mistress called Kusum, an Army officer's widow. The friendship between Gulzari Lal and Kusum is successful because of their common mental behaviour—same ideology and identical temperaments. Their friendship looks as if they are made for each other. That is the reason why Kusum spends most of her time with Gulzari Lal and rules his household. She has free access to the house in the presence of Gulzari Lal's son Vishnu, daughter-in-law, Mala, and the grand-daughter, Priti. They all live in the same house. Gulzari Lal does not feel that there is anything wrong in having a mistress in the house. He thinks that after he returns from office, he needs someone like Kusum who meets his requirements. Kusum takes care of his health, his food, his drinks, his clothes, his servants, etc. She massages his legs. She also shares his bed. She satisfies a man who has been living without a wife for the last ten years. Kusum has become a substitute for a wife in his private life. She wants Gulzari Lal to divorce his wife so that she herself may marry him. For the time being, Gulzari Lal does not feel like divorcing Sarla Devi as this step would bring disrepute to him and it may spoil his business prospects. Kusum even convinces Brij Mohan (Sarla Devi's brother) tempting him with an offer of a bribe. She misleads Sarla Devi into believing that she is a 'spiritual' person and makes her agree to divorce Gulzari Lal. In order to become the sole mistress of Gulzari Lal's house, she drives Mala, Gulzari Lal's daughter-in-law, away with her husband Vishnu by convincing her that it is better if Mala lives separately, away from her father-in-law. This makes Kusum the queen of her house. She recommends Mala's proposal to Gulzari Lal for a separate business. At her instance, Gulzari Lal permits his son to have a factory for making fountain pens at Chandnipet with the collaboration of his friend Joginder Singh. All this Kusum does as her ambition is to become Gulzari Lal's legal wife and to run the administration of the house herself. One can agree with Shahane who says that "the novel *Get Ready for Battle* is not all about battles, fights, quarrels and conflicts. It is a very adroitly designed novel of domestic life and familial relations which are sometimes marked by an intensity of emotions and other times by jealousies and prejudices."[12]

The failure of Sarla Devi at the social level is nothing but a continuation of her failure in her married life, because she does not strike a balance between ideals and reality. Basically, it is her duty to be with her husband and other family members to serve them. Care and love for her husband and concern for the family recede into the background. She goes on for ideals, attending to the needs of other people instead of thinking of her own people. Such contrast of temperament creates in their life a big gulf that is difficult to bridge.

In Delhi, in the name of rehabilitation schemes, the municipal authorities want to evict the people from the *Bundi Busti* where they have been living for the last 15 years. As it is, the living condition of the slum-dwellers in terms of cleanliness is very bad. They live in an unhygienic way. Once "Sarla Devi walked through the narrow lanes between the rows of huts. The earth was streaked with tunnels of dirty water, vegetable waste, and peels were trodden into the mud and scratched up again by mangy dogs and pigs and a few sick chickens" (83). The municipal authorities, instead of improving their health condition by providing extra amenities, prepare a plan to sell the land secretly to Gulzari Lal so that construction of flats may be taken up. Sarla Devi, who lives separately from her husband for the sake of the slum-dwellers, implores him to use his good offices so that the people of Bundi Busti are not evicted. But to her surprise, Gulzari Lal manages matters at the Government level and purchases the land and bribes the labour leader, Ramachandran. In this way, Sarla Devi loses her fight against her husband. But because of the code of conduct by which she lives, she does not give up her struggle and continues to care for the downtrodden people. That is why H.M. Williams points out: "Sarla Devi is the dedicated idealist devoted to the ideals of the *Geeta* and Mahatma Gandhi."[13]

Jhabvala, as an exponent of contemporary Indian scene, depicts the spiritual aspects of Indian life and presents the religious ethos of Indian life. It is also intended to serve as a contrast to the materialistic attitudes of the protagonists. Sarla Devi comes very close to the ideal stage of non-attachment and selfless action, the proclaimed virtues of the *Bhagvad Geeta*. According to the *Bhagvad Geeta*, duty is the disinterested virtuous action performed by Karma Yogins which is known as *Nishkama Karma*.[14] It stresses the need of doing one's duty without looking forward to the fruits thereof. The *Bhagvad Geeta* says that this kind of action will lead to the path of perfection freeing man from the bonds of desires of his heart, consequently finding satisfaction in the real self, within self. The realisation of such an ideal is Sarla Devi's sole aim in life. In pursuit of her ideal, she has left her husband and adopted the teachings of the *Bhagvad Geeta* (Chapter II, verse 38) as summarised in the epigraph of the text:

> Teaching alike pleasure and pain, gain and loss, victory and defeat, then get ready for battle. (105)

However, Sarla Devi is not an ideal embodiment of spiritualism since she, at least in one way, rejects the ideal Hindu wife's way of living by rejecting her husband and her family members. In the true spirit of Lord Krishna's teachings, she keeps herself ready for battle against the corrupt social forces of the society, but unfortunately she fails in her attempts. The reasons for her failure, as H.M. Williams puts it, is the straightforward conflict between "Babbittry"[15] represented by big business and the spiritual values embodied in the novel's "Yogi" figure, a high-principled woman of birth and means who has abandoned her comfortable life for one of extreme austerity and a desire for self-fulfilment; as depicted in Jhabvala's novel is the total failure of communication between the Babbitt and the Yogi.[16]

Jhabvala's Sarla Devi appears to be a social reformer but her extreme reformist fervour and blindness to social reality with reference to modern age indicates her inability to function successfully in any capacity. She is a total failure in her life. On the other hand, Gulzari Lal is an extreme example of a degenerate businessman who represents the decadent modern age. The temperaments of two extremes play a vital role in creating the marital dissonance between wife and husband. Sarla Devi's idealistic attitude clashes with Gulzari Lal's extreme degenerative quality.

The novel ends with Sarla Devi's decision to go to the red-light district to find her brother's prostitute, Tara, and extend sympathy to her as her brother, Brij Mohan, had driven her away from the house. Thus, Sarla Devi gets dissonated from her married life for the "otherworldliness" whereas Gulzari Lal gets dissonated from her for "this worldliness."

## 2 Cross-Cultural Perspective: *Esmond in India* and *A Backward Place*

Jhabvala portrayed the theme of marital dissonance between wife and husband caused by clash between traditionalism and modernism, materialism and idealism respectively, in her novels *The Householder* and *Get Ready for Battle*. She further explores the possibilities of conflicts and disharmony in the conjugal life of couples due to confrontation of East and West cultures in cross-cultural marriages. Such a cultural crisis in respect of East-West encounter occurs in the novel, *Esmond in India.*[17] In many ways this novel is in contrast to *The Householder* in the sense that the married life of Prem and Indu starts off badly but turns happy. The story of *Esmond in India*, like the story of *Get Ready for Battle*, begins off badly and ends up badly with the separation. In *Esmond in India*, Esmond is a Westerner and his wife Gulab is an Indian. It is a cross-cultural marriage. In many ways they are different. Both Esmond and Gulab adamantly cling to their cultural identity in all respects. So, the separation is inevitable. But in *Get Ready for Battle*, Gulzari Lal and Sarla Devi are both Indians. Though their culture is the same, their temperaments are different. Gulzari Lal fails to understand Sarla Devi, and Sarla Devi fails to understand Gulzari Lal. He was modern in every aspect whereas Sarla Devi was an idealist. Her idealism transgresses the limits of realism. There was a gulf between her idealism and realism. Therefore, the marriage is disturbed. In *Esmond in India*, Gulab fails to understand her European husband. But in *A Backward Place*, Judy, a Westerner, understands Mr. Bal, an Indian and compromises with his needs. Thus, there is a contrast between Gulab and Judy; while Bal is successful with Judy, Esmond is a failure with Gulab.

It is traced out that "Jhabvala's novels are full of local colour and clamour, dealing with the young who are inert, romantic and none too-wise, and the old who are cool, calculating and rigid. She describes the head-on collision between the East and the West, and the confusion that follows in the wake of these collisions."[18] In Jhabvala's novels, there is the concept of arranged marriages like the marriage of Prem and Indu. In *The Householder*, marital dissonance results from difference in attitudes. Jhabvala also deals with self-chosen marriages such as the marriage of Gulzari Lal and Sarla Devi in *Get Ready for Battle*. Here also there is dissonance due to temperamental differences. If the dissonance is possible within the marriage of the Indians, then the same problem is definite in cross-cultural marriages. Therefore in her comprehensive portrayal of varieties of discordant marriages, Jhabvala explores cross-cultural marriages as they are more susceptible to dissonance. As we know, the West represents the European tradition and the East is synonymous with India. This essentially intercultural conflict becomes Jhabvala's main pre-occupation because of her personal predicament. In Jhabvala's novels, the East-West relationship is projected in relation to the friction which results when a Westerner comes to India, and tries to get adjusted to the Indian society. During such adjustments, he gets married to an Indian girl. In such marriages, the European finds a flush of excitement and happiness during the initial period of his conjugal life. The moment he begins to notice certain changes, his attitude undergoes a transformation. The weather of India which was bright and sunny to him once, now becomes disgustingly hot and dusty. The people who were affectionate to him once become sentimental now. The food that was once exotic is now regarded as greasy and spicy. The result is that the Westerner feels unhappy and bored. Rudyard Kipling rightly expresses his feelings: "Oh, East is East and West is West and never the twain shall meet." But an idealist feels that they just meet because the search for an optimum point of contact between the two becomes essential for the evaluation of contemporary India. To be frank, in the modern set-up of Indian society, everyone is the product of conflicts between these two cultures, maybe because of mixed marriages, the problems of expatriates and the influence of the West on the Indian way of life. Jhabvala feels that the Indian characters who imitate Western ways of living do not genuinely belong to that tradition and they are unable to shed their Indianness. The Indians who pretend to be modern are tradition-ridden to the core.

The most intriguing aspect of marital dissonance in the novel *Esmond in India* is exemplified in the mixed marriage between persons belonging to the two hemispheres of the world; that is East and West. The Westernised modern upper middle class Indian family is the target of such problems due to conflicting attitudes and interests. For instance, the married life of Esmond and Gulab in the novel is full of conflicts between Eastern and Western patterns of living and the eventual failure of the marriage. There is also another problem in the marriages mixed with the cultures of East and West that "the English are rational and the Indians are emotional. Thus the clash between the two is also a clash between two concepts of culture."[19]

The story of *Esmond in India* is set in post-Independence India. Esmond, an Englishman, earns a living in India teaching Hindi to the wives of foreign embassy officials and giving them expert lectures on Indian art and culture. His wife, Gulab, is an Indian woman. He is tall, handsome and quite impressive. Gulab who was thought an Indian beauty in her college days fell in love with him and married him much against the wishes of her family. Now, she is leading a lackadaisical life of langour in a well-furnished flat. She is visited by her mother every day who also gets Indian food for Gulab. Her sub-conscious thoughts about an ideal marriage are precipitated only when they come into clash with the Western attitudes of Esmond. Gulab's tastes and attitudes are typically Indian. From food to making their son Ravi sleep with her, she has strong Indian attitudes in her. Apart from this, there are clashes in the personalities of Gulab and Esmond. Esmond is a selfish, sophisticated egoist and Gulab is sluttish and unsophisticated. The sharp contrast between the two ways of living and thinking causes awkward and ugly situations in their conjugal life. The easy-going Gulab, with her oriental taste for carrot halwa, spices and other things she preserved for them in the other pots were "gram, tomatoes and potatoes swimming in red curry and chunks of meat soaked in curds" (20) is in sharp contrast to the Western sophistication of Esmond. Her typically Indian bashfulness of high society and indifference towards modern furniture is a glaring contrast to her husband, Esmond, with his innate craze for orderliness, smart and sophisticated society and up-to-date furnishings. Ultimately, he realises the unsuitability of their marriage. His unhappiness creates hatred in him towards everything Indian. He dislikes the Indian climate, the landscape, the people and their way of living. He develops an abnormal and a very negative attitude about India. H.M. Williams rightly observes: "Esmond is perhaps the only completely unattractive villain among all Jhabvala's characters. He hates India but makes a living by teaching Hindi and Indian culture to rich Indian women and English and American tourists. He is also a gigolo."[20]

Esmond and Gulab are two individuals who are as incompatible with each other as their cultures. There is hardly a pleasant meeting between the two. The marriage becomes a battlefield when Esmond insists that Gulab should bring up their son, Ravi, in the European way, keeping him away from the sweet food and without petting or pampering him with sentimental love. But in the absence of Esmond, Gulab simply reverts to Indian ways by providing lavishing sweets and by showering sentimental love on the child. But Gulab never throws herself into confrontation or argument with her husband before others. On the other hand, she supports her husband by telling her mother that they are educating their son according to modern scientific ideas. Gulab's mother frequently interferes with the domestic and administrative affairs of Esmond's family and with most of the things. Like a typical Indian mother-in-law, she ignores the Western ideas of her son-in-law, about food habits to be developed in the child. She suggests:

> He [Ravi] needs such food [good strengthening food cooked in plenty of ghee], and he also needs to have his legs rubbed with oil to make them strong and his hair must be shaved so that it may grow luxuriant, and black shadow must be applied under the eyes to shield them from the strong sun, and in the night he must sleep with his mother so that she may comfort him if he wakes with bad dreams! (148)

According to Ramlal Agarwal, "Jhabvala's understanding of Indian women is greater than her understanding of Indian men. Of all the Indo-Anglian and Anglo-Indian novelists, she also has been able to depict their excessive possessiveness, bickering and domineering nature, their greed and soft-headedness." (35) This is incorporated in the nature of Gulab's mother who wants her grandson under her possession. This behaviour is in total contrast to Esmond's Western approach; and consequently he is irritated not only with Gulab's mother but also with Gulab who encourages her.

The disparity in the cultures, backgrounds and habits of Esmond and Gulab strikes a discordant influence on their marital relationships. Esmond expects, more than anything else, companionship in marriage. He desires a sympathetic, clear, neat, up-to-date, decorative and intimate partner and not a slave. Gulab's unquestioning stoic obedience fails to move him even to compassion. Esmond feels uneasy the moment he looks at his wife with crumpled and torn dress. He observes:

> She was still in the sari which she wore at night; it was crumpled and torn, but she felt at ease in it. (21)

Esmond stops trying to understand Gulab's attitude once and for all. Then he becomes irritable, short-tempered and restless. He sometimes gets sudden outbursts of anger at Gulab whose interests in life do not go beyond sleep and food. His contempt for his wife is such that he revolts at the thought of her. Having been conscious of her presence everywhere in the house, he feels himself trapped and caged:

> She was everywhere; everywhere he felt her—in the heat saturating the air which clung to him and enveloped him as in a sheath of perspiration; in the sugarcane juice, which the people in the streets were drinking and which he could almost taste, filled with dust and germs and too much sweetness; in the faint but penetrating smell of over-ripe fruit; everywhere, she was everywhere, and he felt himself stifling in her softness and her warmth. (217)

Gulab adopted a fanatic, orthodox Indian way of life. "She [Gulab] has a sensuous, instinctive awareness of reality and acts habitually by instinct rather than by ratiocination."[21] Thus she lacks understanding about the changed times. As a Westerner, Esmond is not in a position either to understand or to appreciate her passive, obedient and submissive nature. As a result, the beast in him surfaces and he pinches and slaps her, forgetting his sophistication. He wonders at his own behaviour:

> To his horror he found himself wanting to seize her again and tear at her flesh and even to bite into her, to let his teeth sink deep into her soft body; to hurt her till he got some human response from her, even if it was nothing more than a cry of pain. (216)

The only comfort and solace for Esmond is the company of Betty and her Englishness. "He always, whenever he felt particularly oppressed by Gulab, went to see Betty. Her flat was so light, modern, and airy; she herself so light, modern and airy. Being with her was almost as good as being in England—which was the one place where he wanted most passionately to be." (50) Esmond feels alienated in India. His feelings of homelessness and the absence of a sympathetic friend fill him with a sense of insecurity and loss. He feels like returning to England for a sense of relief. But he does not go anywhere, as his financial position does not allow him to. So, "Esmond in India is neither about Esmond alone, nor about India only, but about the social segment that functions as a setting for Esmond's experience."[22] Shakuntala, Har Dayal's daughter, who is influenced very much by Western style of life unfortunately, got entangled with Esmond who leads the team as a guide to a group from the Western Women's Organisation. Har Dayal introduces his pretty idealistic young daughter to Esmond in order to introduce her to the rich cosmopolitan circles. "Shakuntala, a naive, self-willed romantic with her head turned by her father's flattery and illusion that he and his smart friends are in the van of freedom and enlightenment, succumbs with pathetic ease to Esmond's experienced charm."[23] Temporarily dropping his cynical and hard-boiled English mistress, Betty, Esmond seduces Shakuntala on a trip to Agra. Shakuntala speaks to Esmond in a passionate way:

> Esmond, I know you are married and also have a child, but I tell you all this means nothing to me. (192)

Betty attempts to strife the affairs between Esmond and Shakuntala but she starts laughing outrightly watching Esmond stand "deflated into a small ridiculous figure."[24]

Gulab also suffers from a feeling of being caged in her own house. The presence of her husband in the house creates a tense atmosphere and she always lives in dread of her husband. Though she desperately tries to adjust herself in her husband's home, she has not changed her life style. Gulab and her mother are very much attached to each other. Laurie Sucher misses the basic psychological struggle of Gulab and Esmond in her observation about Jhabvala's fiction. She points out: "this novel, *Esmond in India*, contains one of Ruth Jhabvala's most positive depiction of a mother and daughter relationship. Esmond's mismatched wife, Gulab, their toddler, Ravi, and Gulab's mother, Uma, enjoy an intimate domesticity that lends the charm and a tenderness to this novel."[25] Such a mother-daughter relationship may be considered charming, if the daughter is a widow or separated from her husband. But Uma's interference is a major contributory factor for the dissonance of married life between Esmond and Gulab. Gulab knows everything in terms of her behaviour. Jhabvala observes that in spite of the stupidity and sluggishness, there is genuineness in her nature which is at once amusing and pathetic. She accepts her position with an attitude of resignation. From the Indian point of view, one can understand Gulab's languorous way of life, her liking of spicy food and her feeling of discomfort in a smartly-furnished flat which seems to restrict her freedom of movement. She feels a sense of restlessness and alienation in such modern flats:

> Gulab, lying on the floor, felt as comfortable as she ever felt in that flat. It was not really convenient to her way of living. In her mother's house she had been used to vast rooms and little furniture, so that she had been able to lie on an old stringbed in the middle of an otherwise empty room, floating as on a great sea of cracked marble flooring under a high, high ceiling fretted—a sky with clouds—with flaking frescoes. But here, in her husband's flat, she was hemmed in by furniture, there was no room to lie down, no room to move at her ease. Oh yes, everybody said what nice furniture it was and how clever Esmond was to make so much of that small flat. He had utilised every corner, fitted in divans and shelves and coffee-tables, all very low and modern and, so they said, attractive. But Gulab could not see any purpose for so much furniture; it only prevented one from being comfortable. (20)

Gulab's concept of marriage is orthodox: she feels that marriage should provide her security. Though it is the husband's right to treat his wife as he likes, it is also his duty to see that she is safe in his house. But, her servant, taking advantage of their marital dissonance, tries to molest her. He enters her room and fumbling with the words, "My dearie, my dearie." "For a moment his hand lay on her flesh and she looked down at it because she could not believe it, though she felt it there" (259). Thus, her personal honour is assaulted by the servant. She feels that she has no use of a husband who cannot protect her honour.[26] Esmond fails in his duty. Gulab's sense of security is shattered and she feels that in no way she should be bound to marriage. So, he is no more her husband; nor is she his wife. Though her mother and uncle [mother's brother, Ram Nath] have been suggesting to her to leave her husband's house because of the incompatibility between wife and husband, Gulab has been resisting it. Ram Nath opines once, "When these differences go very deep, it is better for husband and wife to part because otherwise they will begin to hate one another and that is very ugly" (172). Now the time has come to leave her husband's house.

Thus, she takes the final decision and walks out leaving the doors unlocked:

> She left the door open; the flat meant nothing to her anymore; it was dead, finished, so how could she be expected to shut the door and lock it and worry about Esmond's possessions. (261)

*Esmond in India* (1957) was Ruth Jhabvala's first novel of expatriation. In this novel, there is only one expatriate character and that is Esmond. Esmond married an Indian girl. The marriage between Esmond and Gulab broke because of cross-cultural conflicts. Otherwise Esmond was happy in India. In general he had no problems with Indians but he had problems with his wife because of the clash in the personal and domestic maintenance of two different cultures. Jhabvala was also personally happy during this period though she is also an expatriate settled in India after her marriage. Since then she has been tirelessly exploring the sensibility of Western expatriates in India. Her personal history of displacement has been transformed into a fictional land of the spirit in which her protagonists try to place themselves, feel at home and rarely succeed. She told an interviewer in 1974: "I was practically born a displaced person, and all, any of us ever wanted was a travel document and a residential permit. One just didn't care as long as one was allowed to live somewhere."[27] Her marriage with Cyrus Jhabvala, a young Parsi architect, made her leave Britain and come to India with her husband in 1951. Her encounter with India created abundant joy and pleasure to her. About her life in India she said:

> It came about instinctively. I was enraptured. I felt I understood India so well. I loved everything . . . perhaps I loved it . . . because

> of my being Jewish. The Indian family life, the humour, was closer to the Jewish world I know than the Anglo-Saxon world.[28]

Jhabvala's first stage of artistic experience which lasted for about nine years during which time she never left India but experienced an increasing delight of love. She described India as a "Paradise on earth."[29] Her love of India can be seen in her early novels, *To Whom She Will* and *The Nature of Passion*.

In 1960 Jhabvala returned to Europe for the first time after 1951 and the trip was to have a profound effect on her attitude to India. In her later works, especially in *A Backward Place*,[30] Jhabvala created numerous European characters and developed increasing dissatisfaction with India. Jhabvala, like many of her European characters, found that she was strapped to a wheel that carried her through the stages she believes all Europeans who visit India inevitably pass through. She explains these stages in an essay entitled 'Myself in India,' which introduced her third collection of short stories, *An Experience of India*:

> There is a cycle that Europeans—by Europeans I mean all Westerners, including Americans—tend to pass through. It goes like that: first stage, tremendous enthusiasm—everything Indian is marvellous; second stage, everything Indian not so marvellous; third stage, everything Indian abominable. For some people it ends there, for others the cycle renews itself and goes on. I have been through it so many times that now I think of myself as strapped to a wheel that goes round and round and sometimes I'm up and sometimes I'm down. When I meet other Europeans, I can usually tell after a few moments' conversation at what stage of the cycle they happen to be.[31]

Eventually, she felt the need to escape that wheel, and in 1975, soon after the publication of *Heat and Dust*, Jhabvala moved to New York. But, according to Ralph J. Crane, she cannot escape from India in the sense "the wheel . . . is as much the wheel of disinheritance and expatriatism as the wheel of European fortune in India. The latter is one which may be escaped, the former is perhaps one which cannot. Without wishing to reach too deeply into the can of biographical criticism, an awareness of Jhabvala's almost unique position as a disinherited writer cannot be ignored, as her essay, 'Myself in India' makes clear. Her disinheritance, and the influence it has had and continues to have on her writing is discussed by a number of critics."[32]

Basically, it appears that Jhabvala merged with India—Indian concept of life, Indian philosophy, Indian social, political and economic aspects and systems. She has lived in India for most of her adult life. Her husband is an Indian and her children are Indian. She was angry at most of the Westernised Indians as they maintained the life of the hypocrites. They were not true representatives of India. They gave an impression to the Western society that they really represent India but it was not so. There are people in poor condition, people living in the joint family system, people struggling hard for bread and butter. Jhabvala involved herself with the people of India in all aspects and she expressed her sense of individuality and desire in her essay, 'Myself in India':

> Of course, this cannot go on indefinitely and in the end I am bound to lose—if only at the point where my ashes are immersed in the Ganges to the accomplishment of Vedic hymns, and then who will say that I have not truly merged with India. (10)

Jhabvala's novels are primarily concerned with problems of women in marriage, in love and in inter-personal relationships. In the novel *A Backward Place*, however, she the synthesizes these problems with that of expatriates. Twice expatriated herself from Germany to England and from England to India, Jhabvala is obviously fascinated by the problems of expatriates. *A Backward Place* is the only one of her novels so far which can be said to dwell exclusively on this subject. If R.K Narayan's settings are in Malgudi, Jhabvala's settings are in Delhi. Of course, there is a difference in these settings; R.K. Narayan's Malgudi is an imaginary place and the place has been developing in the mind of the writer from a small hamlet to the city of today; but Jhabvala's Delhi in her novels is not imaginary. It is the real place.

That is the reason she portrays in the novel the backwardness of modern India through the feelings of the characters of expatriates. *A Backward Place* deals less with Indian characters and more with Europeans. H.M. Williams observes: "It is the nearest that Jhabvala has yet come to such novels of East-West confrontation as E.M. Forster's *A Passage to India* and Raja Rao's *The Serpent and the Rope*. She rigidly excludes the political, racial, metaphysical and poetic approaches of Forster and Rao, and sticks firmly to her 'forte' of exploring the private lives of a few women in middle-class Delhi. The three women are all expatriates, and their common problem is coming to terms with the 'backward place' which is modern India."[33]

*A Backward Place* articulates several shades of Jhabvala's art, her emotional and intellectual responses towards India. While leading her own comfortable life in the four walls of an air-conditioned room, Jhabvala as an artist cannot get away from what she believes to be an overwhelming aspect of the hard reality of India:

> All the time I know myself to be on the back of this great animal of poverty and backwardness. It is not possible to pretend otherwise. Or rather, one does pretend, but retribution follows.[34]

The problems that India, as a stark reality or as a spiritual reality, presented to the Europeans evoke different responses. The reactions may assume the forms of affirmation, or negation or ambivalence. All these areas of emotive and intellectual responses to this country are endowed with fictional art in *A Backward Place*. Jhabvala is also critical of the validity of the Westernised Indians' attitudes to the problems of their country. Their way of life is:

> Everything they say, all that lively conversation round the buffet table, is not promoted by anything they really feel strongly about but by what they think they ought to feel strongly about.[35]

Jhabvala seems dissatisfied with this unreality in the sophisticated, Westernised Indians' attitude to India. She feels more at home with the semi-educated, but deeply involved Indian joint families which breathe a genuine get-togetherness. About joint family life in India, Jhabvala says:

> There is actually something very restful about this mode of social intercourse and certainly holds more pleasure than the synthetic social life led by Westernised Indians. It is also more adapted to the Indian climate which invites one to be absolutely relaxed in mind and body, to do nothing, to think nothing, just to feel to be. I have in fact enjoyed sitting around like that for on end.[36]

Ruth Prawer Jhabvala's main forte as the creative writer after the publication of *Esmond in India* (1957), is the interaction and conflict that she shows between the cultures of the East and the West. This distinct quality is as much valid in her other writings as it is valid in her novel *A Backward Place*. Her reaction to this interaction is depicted in her autobiographical essay, "Myself in India." She writes, "I have lived in India for most of my adult life. My husband is Indian and so are my children. I am not, and less so every year."[37]

In a way, Jhabvala's ambivalence towards India is a pointer to certain flaws which are evident in her novel *A Backward Place*. Her three European characters, 'expatriates' as they are called in the novel, can be classified into two categories. Etta, a Hungarian expatriate, and Clarissa, an English woman, can be put in the first category. They wanted to cling to their culture and want to go back. But they are retained in India unquestionably for various reasons and the result is that they lose their identity at both the ends. The third character, Judy, who comes under the second category, has a conflict, struggle and marital dissonance with her Indian husband for various reasons. But at the end of the novel, she surrenders to her husband's will by following him to Bombay.

Etta, the first expatriate in the first category, is a Hungarian beauty, married and divorced three times. Her attitude towards marriage is the characteristic attitude of the West which is entirely different from the Eastern attitude. Marriage and divorce are not serious subjects to her. She is impulsive and passionate. Her first marriage had been to an Indian student whom she had met in Vienna: the handsomest, most cultured, charming boy one could imagine. She had gone with him for dancing in all the nicest cafes. But, once back in India he is turned out for the reason that he is attached to a most uncultured family in India. She considers his family as the typical educated but uncultured family. Delhi city is dull and backward. She calls her land of exile as the primitive society. She tells her friend Judy on her first visit to her flat "in this primitive society, that's no reason why we should submit to their primitive morality" (5). She wages a bitter war against both India and the spectre of approaching age which seems to her to be different aspects of the same antagonist. She tells Judy, "Don't you know that the Indian sun has been put specially into the sky to ruin our complexions?" (7) Etta has a superior attitude to the world and asks Judy to break off her relationship with her husband Bal. She tells Judy, "Marriages, my dear, are made to be broken, that's one of the rules of modern civilization" (5). Etta always interferes in the personal and domestic affairs of Judy and passes on certain undesired, unasked for and unwanted suggestions to her. At one stage, Etta tells Judy, "Judy, you must leave him [her husband] and get out. You are just rotting here. Look at you in that thing—Judy looked down at herself, at the sari which she mostly wore now-a-days—and your hair too and—ugh,—you are awful" (5-6). She is not happy with Judy because Judy is the breadwinner and her husband Bal, is a wanderer. She asks Judy to leave the job too. She tells her, "I hate to see you going on and on like this. Married to that awful—well, he is awful, don't expect me to mince words. I never, never mince words, you know that; Judy did. 'If at least he were earning decently and could make some sort of life for you here, but not even that! It's you who have to go out to work" (7). With such attitudes, Etta divorced her first husband, then Guppy (Gupta) and Jumperwala became desperate. A. Jaganmohana Chari observes: "the absence of love and innocence in her world make it an ugly caricature."[37] She always considers India as a backward place. Dr. Franz Hochstadt, an Economist from Germany, was happy with India's spiritual and intellectual aspects. When he praises India, Etta reacts angrily and bursts out:

> 'Oh do stop it, Franz!' Etta interrupted. 'India, India, India, all the time, as if there was anything interesting to be said! One has the misfortune to be here, well all right, let's leave at that, but why do we have to keep on torturing ourselves by talking about it?' (28)

Another Westerner stranded in India is Clarissa, an English woman of good family who declares that she, unlike Etta, is in India out of conviction and idealism. She is an artist *manqué*, unmarried and even after idyllic beauty available in plenty in India, but not able to get at it. She expresses her yearning to be back to her beloved mountains—Nature. Actually Clarissa belongs to the sort, in Sudhir Bannerjee's words:

> she must have come out to India first, spurred on by Romain Rolland and the Light of Asia and the Everyman edition of the *Bhagvad Geeta*, and intent on a quest in which notions of Soul and God played a prominent, if vague part; and how valiantly she had kept up this quest, or at least the pretence of it, though she was getting older year by year and lonelier, and more ridiculous, and Soul and God perhaps no nearer. (94)

This beautifully sums up the noble abstracts which had drawn Clarrisa away from her position into the placid world of the peasants of India where she had neither talent nor a common factor to fit in. "India is her ideal, her lovely land, the land of Vivekananda and Ramakrishna she has read about in dingy old England. She found to her bitter cost that a great gulf lies between holy India and the India of reality."[38] Her life which was to have been the pursuit of metaphysical wisdom, has turned out to be a struggle with the climate, predatory landlords and the need to make ends meet. Her peculiar situation arises because she is a pseudo-liberal, trying hard to live up to liberal ideals that she does not hold on to deep down within herself. Her comments on India's social system resemble the nostalgic, sentimental views of medievalists who take no account of personal and psychological damage done to the Indian citizen who must suffer the adverse effects of the institution of caste:

> I'm very very anti-untouchability and all that, I think it's simply horrible, but I can see all the same that there's something beautiful about the caste system. Beautiful and right. Every man in his own rank, doing his own work, there's a divine harmony there which is entirely lacking in the West today. (91)

There are two other Westerners in the novel, Dr. Franz Hochstadt and his wife Frieda Hochstadt, short-term residents in Delhi on a University exchange programme. They appreciate India:

> For the newcomer in India perhaps one of the most interesting aspects is the correlation—and here I have in mind not only physical facts but also intellectual and spiritual ones—the correlation of the old and the new, of what has been and what is. (28)

Most of these Westerners, however, are victims of marital dissonance. The marital dissonance between Judy and her husband Bal, for instance, is not simply a result of the East-West encounter, it is in fact rooted in the clash of their temperaments. H.M. Williams aptly analyses and concludes: "the marriage of Bal and Judy is difficult not because of the difference in race so much as because of the clash in their temperaments between the dreamer [Bal] and the pragmatist [Judy]."[39] Here Judy is an English girl married to an Indian actor, Bal, who is not exactly a success. Judy believes in pragmatism whereas Bal believes in unquenchable optimism. Basically, English people are rationalists; they act according to reason and logic and take decisions meticulously, covering every aspect in life whereas Indians like Bal think in terms of emotional and optimistic aspects and believe in dreams. Judy, being practical by nature, thinks in terms of pros and cons and maintains the balance of mind and tongue both in thought and actions.

The novel focuses on the relationship between Judy and Bal. Judy met Bal in London where he came as an Indian delegate to a conference of International Youth. She fell in love with his handsome face and his cheerful manner. Her home in England was cheerless. She was impressed very much by Bal's spirits. So, she married him. She settled in a low middle class joint family in Delhi. She is blessed with two children—son Prithvi and daughter Gita. Judy is the bread-winner, works in the organization called 'Culture Dais' as the Assistant to the General Secretary, Mr. Sudheer Bannerjee. Mrs. Kaul is the honorary secretary of the organization. Bal, a B.A. degree holder calls himself an artist and he is connected with radio, stage and movies. Once, Prithvi, Judy's little son, has fever and wants his father to stay with him, but Bal wants to go out to meet his friend, a film-star of Bombay, Mr. Kishan Kumar. For Bal, Kishan Kumar who is available in Delhi is more important than the feverish condition of his son. Prithvi appeals to his father with the words, "stay and play with me" (22). Prithvi demands water with ice. Judy wants her husband to go out and fetch ice:

> 'Get the ice,' she said. 'It is very important for me to keep up my contacts. Without contact you can't succeed in my line!' 'Are you getting it or not?' (25)

She pursues him in the street, catching him by the sleeve, asking him to do his duty as father first. He at last yields and brings ice for the child.

Bal has strong hopes of getting a role in the film world with the help of Kishan Kumar. V.A. Shahane observes: "Bal's irrepressible enthusiasm, however amateurish and childlike it seems, symbolizes an element of hope in a distracted land, a backward place." (80) He is being tempted easily with Kishan Kumar's invitation. Whenever he meets, Kishan Kumar asks Bal to visit Bombay to get the position of the Head of the production unit of the films. He is in Delhi without work. Judy, with the cooperation of Mr. Sudheer at the 'Culture Dais' and at the instance of Bal, moves a proposal to start a unit called 'Professional Theatre' so that Bal could be employed for Judy has been struggling with the meagre income to run the house with two children. Besides this, she has been saving some money in the bank for the future of the children. Now, the savings have come to Rs. 725. At last the 'Professional Theatre' plan has been approved by Mrs. Kaul, with the keen interest of Mr. Sudheer, but Bal abruptly announces that he has nothing to do with the theatre:

> 'I don't want anything to do with their theatre. Let them leave me alone.'
>
> Judy said, 'But it was you who wanted the theatre!.'
>
> Bal replied, 'That was before they insulted me.' (144)

This sudden change of attitude in Bal disturbed Judy. Basically, she didn't want him to go to Bombay. She had no faith in Kishan Kumar's production unit; and she knew that once Bal was in Bombay, in the vicinity of film studios and stars and in the company of all the other people hanging and hoping around them, he would soon forget about his family and concentrate only on having a good time with his friends (125-26). On the one hand Judy is not ready for Bal's proposals to shift to Bombay; and on the other Bal is not ready to continue his stay in Delhi and to work with 'Culture Dais' since he has been insulted by Etta at the picnic party hosted by Dr. Franz Hochstadt.

> Judy wants to know how has he been insulted. He said, "'I can't laugh when insults are offered to me. This just not possible for me.' She [Etta] insulted me."
>
> 'But how, how?'
>
> 'You and me, both of us. She said I make you work for me, that I can't earn enough to keep you—.' He clenched his fists in fury. . . . His voice went very high pitched and ended on something like a sob. 'How often I have said I don't want you to go to any office! How I begged and begged you not to—.'
>
> 'But I like it,' Judy exclaimed.
>
> 'You like it. But my position, this has never occurred to you, how it looks to others that I, your husband, allow you to go out to work, what a disgrace that is to me. . . .'
>
> '. . . in England everybody goes out to work, all the married women and everyone,' Judy said.

> '. . . This is not England! Here do you see any of our ladies going out? Do you see my sister-in-law [brother's wife, Shanti] leaving her home to go and work among strangers? Do you think my brother would ever allow?' (145-46)

As a matter of fact, Judy is deeply concerned with Bal's job. She is a worrying type. Even in her sleep she talks about it. Once she woke up from her sleep and was talking to herself, "You'd better get a job" (110). Apart from Bal's job her children's future is also a matter of concern. Now, they are growing up and they need more money for education, for medicines, for marriages in future. Her savings of Rs. 725 are very limited. She is also worried that if she loses her job at Culture Dais, what will be her fate because Bal is of no use looking after domestic affairs. Judy wanted to be realistic and absolutely serious towards her life with Bal and children. For her growing worries, she consulted Mr. Sudheer, who in turn cynically replied, "'Look, Judy, you have been alright for these ten years, isn't it? Then why not for another ten?' She cried suddenly in anguish, 'But he's never had a proper job! Never earned enough to keep a flea'" (111). On the other side, Mr. Kaul, Honorary Secretary of Culture Dais was planning to replace Judy in order to accommodate another girl whose parents are known to him. Moreover, there are pressures from Bal for money. Bal wants an advance of Rs. 200 from her savings. Judy refuses: "How can I manage on less? Look, the fare alone, even though I shall go third class, will cost me sixty rupees return. And then I must have some money in Bombay—I have to eat and go to various places." (123).

Bal's plan is to go to Bombay first, then call on his family members. Judy is not prepared to part with Bal as she loves him. When Judy refuses his repeated requests, he gets angry and says, "Why are you like this? I am trying so hard to advance in my profession and you want only to hold me back. A wife should give encouragement to her husband, not hold him back!" (125) Later he cools down and again he pleads with Judy in tempting words. Then, Sudheer asks Judy to convince Bal to drop the

Bombay proposal. Judy wails, "You don't know how I've argued with him and quarrelled and everything, but he won't listen! He just won't!" (158)

Actually, Bal should be considered very lucky to have a wife like Judy. In spite of her Western background, she maintains a family life in the Eastern style. She tries her best to neutralise the marital differences or dissonance with her husband. Yasmine Gooneratne rightly observes: "Bal is treated by his creator [and by his wife Judy] like an appealing child." (175) She has abundant patience and tolerance. But it is a fact that the conjugal life of Bal and Judy suffers from incompatibility because of conflicts in their mental attitudes. Judy is a down-to-earth realist and her husband is the centre of her life along with their two children. Her husband is a compulsive dreamer. Bal's childlike enthusiasm and blind hope in a desolate and backward place makes her mentally tired. She is disgusted with quarrels, discussions, arguments and counter-arguments with her husband. She also gets exhausted with Bal. In an angry mood, one day, she leaves the house and rushes straight out of the courtyard into the street. She goes a long way, then she turns back to look at the house where she found her husband sitting on the string cot. She "caught the expression of surprise and sorrow on his face, as he sat there on the string cot and then she was off again" (87). On the way back to home, she meets Bhuaji and her two children. Forgetting the Western style of life with aggressive turn, she thinks of the children and the husband again like an Indian wife and, unlike Sarla Devi in *Get Ready for Battle*, meets Bal and cools down. In order to overcome this problem, she turns to the Indian epic, the *Ramayana*. She feels like following the path of Seeta who followed Rama everywhere. So Judy, while sitting at Moghel park, takes a decision to go to Bombay as Bal desires. Judy tells Bal 'Let us go to Bombay.' Her sudden and abrupt decision makes Bal very happy. With his family and Bhuaji, they reach the railway station platform to leave for Bombay. Thus the novel ends with the departure of Bal, Judy, their children and Bhuaji to

Bombay and also the departure of Sudheer Bannerji to Calcutta to join the literacy mission. The Hochstadts had already left for Germany, Etta and Clarissa, who had initially considered India as a backward place, decide to stay together in India in a flat.

Throughout the novel, thus, there is disagreement, dissatisfaction, incompatibility, and a clash of pragmatism and optimism between Bal and Judy, because Bal is a freak and an incorrigible dreamer while Judy is an action-oriented realistic person. But at the end of the novel, peaceful coexistence and harmony results due to the inner resolve and determination of a woman. This makes Jhabvala's novel *The Householder* to move into the stream of togetherness where Prem and Indu, like Bal and Judy, psychologically join and move together obviously with a belief that life is nothing but an adjustment.

### 3 Marriage without Love and Love without Marriage: *Heat and Dust*

Ruth Prawer Jhabvala is counted as a modern writer of contemporary India. She is neither brutally frank like Nirad C. Chaudhuri, nor traditional in her themes like Mulk Raj Anand or R.K. Narayan. She has chosen for her a subject matter, the most vitally modern—the aspect of marriage without love and love without marriage in contemporary Indian life. She has been writing for the past forty years but her eighth novel *Heat and Dust*[40] is the one which has Indian situations and settings. She won the famous Booker Prize for this novel in London in 1975. That's why H.S. Mahle considers her as the novelist belonging "to the category of manufacturers rather than to that of growers of books."[41]

The issue of marriage without love and love without marriage is one of the burning problems in modern India. Jhabvala dealt with the theme in her novels. The theme of *Heat and Dust* is on a different plane in the sense that both the hero and the heroine, Douglas and Olivia, are from the same culture, same religion, same social and educational background. Still there is marital dissonance. The reason for their dissatisfaction is

Olivia's emotional dissatisfaction. They are married but they do not have psychological love between them. They are not made for each other. A woman's happiness depends not just on providing everything in terms of comforts, luxuries but there is something beyond materialistic comforts that she needs. This affection one can get only with love but not with money or material. This love Olivia lacks, so there is dissatisfaction and that leads to marital dissonance. Olivia's is a different character compared with other characters of Jhabvala. In *Get Ready for Battle*, for instance, attitudinal differences between Gulzari Lal and Sarla Devi lead to total separation whereas in *The Householder* and *A Backward Place*, the differences between Prem and Indu and Bal and Judy respectively do finally lead to a sense of coexistence. Again, in *Esmond in India*, the marital dissonance results from cross-cultural conflicts. Here in the novel *Heat and Dust*, the problem of marriage without love and love without marriage is due to emotional and destructive sexual desire with which the heroine of the novel, Olivia who is vulnerable, sensitive and passionate is possessed. She is an unholy wife to her holy husband, Douglas, the Assistant Collector at Satipur town in Central India.

Olivia's India, as reflected in her diary and letters, is the India of the early thirties. *Heat and Dust* is a novel of two women, Olivia, the heroine and the narrator, whose name has not been mentioned anywhere in the novel. The story is about the two English women and their life in India 25 years before and after independence. Mrs. Beth Crawford, the Collector's wife at Satipur is the young narrator's auntie, and Miss Tessie, Beth's sister, is the narrator's grandmother. Tessie married Douglas after he got a divorce from Olivia. The narrator is Tessie's granddaughter who comes to India with a bunch of Olivia's letters to unravel the mystery of Olivia's existence and the dismal oddities of her life. The narrator wants to know about Olivia, her way of life, her friends, her parties, her escapades which finally culminate in her elopement with the young Muslim Nawab. The narrator visits India in the Seventies, that is, after half a century, to investigate the details related to Olivia.

The title of the novel, *Heat and Dust*, symbolises the psychological state of the characters involved. The first reference to the title occurs in Olivia's way of life, in fact, the first phase of it when, as the wife of Douglas, she lives in a large and dull house. She feels bored and lonely in that spacious house:

> The rest of the time Olivia was alone in her big house with all doors and windows shut to keep out the heat and dust. (14)

The heat and dust thus stands for an aspect of India. Olivia finds time only in the evenings or on Sundays when she happens to meet a handful of stereotype Anglo-Indian families in town. They are Mrs. Minnies, the wife of Major Minnies, the political agent to advise the Nawab, Mrs. Beth Crawford, the wife of Mr. Crawford, the Collector of Satipur town, and Mrs. Saunders, the wife of Dr. Saunders, the British Medical Superintendent of Khatm town. In order to spend her time, Olivia reads books and plays the piano but she feels that the days are long. Douglas is extremely busy with his work in the district.

> He [Douglas] always got up at crack of dawn—very quietly, for fear of waking her—to ride out on inspection before the sun got too hot. After that he went to the courthouse and to his office and was usually too rushed to come home again till late in the evening and then always with files. By that time Olivia woke up, the servants had cleaned the house and let down all the blinds and shutters. The entire day was her own. In London she had loved having hours and hours to herself—she had always thought of herself as a very introspective person. But here she was beginning to dread these lonely days locked up with the servants who padded around on naked feet and respectfully waited for her to want something. (17-18)

Douglas is always busy with his official duties. He has little time to spare for his wife who is all the time waiting for him. He is a workaholic. His superiors applaud him for his sincerity and honesty and the way he handles the administration in the district:

> Douglas worked like a Trojan and never ceased to be calm and controlled, so that he was very much esteemed both by his colleagues and by the Indians. He was upright and just. (1)

The fortitude with which Englishmen bear the heat while on duty in the plains is related to the strength, tenacity and moral uprightness of their character. This, in fact, is one aspect of the general image of an Anglo-Indian. Douglas is the prime example of such an image in the novel. His wife loves him very much "for his imperturbability, his English solidness and strength, his manliness" (116). Douglas is worried very much about Olivia as he finds her bored and out of mood. He feels that the effect of the heat and dust on Anglo-Indian women is such they often become irritable and quarrelsome. "Douglas for instance, blames the Indian heat and dust for increasing tension building up between Olivia and himself."[42]

The young Nawab of Khatm invites all the Anglo-Indian officials along with their wives for a dinner party. Mr. Harry is a close house guest to the Nawab Sahib. Douglas and Olivia also attend the dinner party. For Olivia, all the officials look dull and boring except her husband. "Only Douglas was different. She stole a look at him: Yes, he was right. As always, he was sitting up very straight; his nose was straight, so was his forehead; his evening jacket fitted impeccably. He was noble and fair" (16). Such a favourable view of Douglas' appearance is not restricted to Olivia who, being his wife, may be partial. Even in Harry's opinion, Douglas distinguished himself from others in the party. Surprisingly, the host, Nawab's eyes rest on Olivia. She allows his gaze to study her while she pretends not to notice. She likes the behaviour of the Nawab, the style of his conversation, the way he receives the guests, the arrangement of the dinner with long tables decorated with flowers, candlebars, the variety of the dishes, pomegranates, pineapples, crystallized fruits, little golden bowls, etc. "She felt she had, at last in India, come to the right place" (15). Olivia likes the way the Nawab looks at her when she first comes in. "His eyes had lit up—he checked himself immediately, but she had seen it and realised that here at last was one person in India to be interested in her the way she was used to." (17)

After the party Olivia's behaviour changes significantly. She feels better about being alone in the house all day. She develops a sense of hope that the Nawab will call on her as she experiences the soft and friendly behaviour of the Nawab in the dinner party. Now she starts dressing in a different way "in one of her cool, pastel muslins" and waits for the Nawab. To her surprise, four days after the dinner party, the Nawab Sahib visits. She says, "Why Nawab Sahib, what a lovely surprise. She got up to greet him, holding out both hands to him in welcome" (18). That evening, Douglas finds Olivia so excited for the first time. Olivia reports to Douglas the visit of the Nawab: "he had his doubts—but seeing how gay she was, how glad, he decided it was all right. She was lonely, and it was decent of the Nawab to have called on her" (19).

Jhabvala very scrupulously observes the behaviour of the Anglo-Indians and the effect of heat and dust on them. They often become irritable and quarrelsome. The only escape for them is to go to some hill-station like Simla. But the men posted at far-off places would not avail of such easy options. They would instead remain at their posts of duty and devote themselves to their work. Thus, Douglas, Saunders, Major Minnies and other Anglo-Indian officials do not think of going to any hill-resorts. However, the option is open for the ladies and they generally make use of it to spend half the year at Simla. Douglas ascribes Olivia's irritability to the climate:

> He sucked at his pipe in rather a pleased way which made her cry out sharply: "Don't do that!" He took it out of his mouth and stared in surprise. "I hate you with that thing, Douglas," she explained.
>
> Although he didn't understand why, he saw that she was upset so he laid it aside. "I don't like it much myself," he said frankly. There was a pause. She stopped sewing, stared into space; her pretty lower lip was sulky. (39)

Douglas decides to send his wife to Simla with the other European ladies but Olivia's refusal to go to Simla is beautifully illustrated in the following passage:

> He said, "It'll be all right once you get to the hills. It's the heat, darling, that's getting you."
>
> "I know it is . . . but when will you be able to get away?"
>
> "Never mind about me. It's you we have to take care of. I was talking to Beth [wife of the collector, Mr. Crawford] today. They're thinking of leaving on the 17th, and I said kindly to book a berth for you at the same time. It's the Kalka Mail—an overnight journey, but it won't be too bad, I promise you." He was so pleased with his arrangement that it didn't occur to him she could be anything else. "It's another four hours up the mountains but what a journey! You'll love it. The scenery, not to speak of the change of climate—"
>
> "You don't for one moment think that I would go without you!"
>
> "Beth Crawford will be there, and Mary Minnies. They'll take care of you." He gave one look at her face and said: "That's just silly, Olivia. Mother spent four months away from Father every year for years on end. From April to September. She didn't like it either, but you're in a district, that's the way it has to be."
>
> "I'm not going," Olivia said, sitting up very straight and looking at him very straight too. Then she said, "The Nawab wants to give a party for us."
>
> "Very kind of him," Douglas said drily. He picked up his pipe again to knock it against the fender.
>
> "Yes it is rather," Olivia said. "He sent Harry over specially to ask us."
>
> "It's not every day that royalty throws parties for junior officers."
>
> "No, but I expect he's as bored as we are with our seniors"
>
> "We are?"
>
> "I am." (39-40)

This conversation between Douglas and Olivia makes it clear that marital dissonance in them is at peak level. Douglas plans something for Olivia but she has different ideas. He wants to provide her a comfortable stay at Simla but she is not ready and reacts in a negative way. This lack of mutual understanding and settlement strikes a chord of dissonance between them. Olivia realises this.

> "Why are we quarreling?" she asked.
>
> He considered her question for a moment and then came up with his reasoned reply: "Because the climate is making you irritable. That's only natural, it happens to all of us. And of course it's much worse for you having to stay home all day with nothing to do. That's why I want you to go away." After a moment he added "You don't think I like it any better than you, do you." Then she collapsed completely and could only be held up by his strong arms. She said she'd be bored, she'd be irritable, she'd be hot, she'd quarrel with him—all right! But please not to send her away from him. (40)

Olivia does not like to go because of her growing involvement and interest in the Nawab. She pleads with her husband not to send her away to Simla. Her growing attraction towards the Nawab leads her gradually away from her family. K.P.K. Menon rightly remarks: "The attraction is mutual and culminates in her elopement with him."[43] It is true that Douglas and Olivia are married and they are wife and husband but their marital life is in disarray. It is understood that Olivia is sentimental, emotional whereas Douglas is a man with a practical bent of mind. Actually, they require mutual understanding and settlement. It is conspicuously absent and "this dissonance may be owing to different attitudes towards life."[44] Douglas does everything for Olivia, he is so busy and he does not have the time to talk to his wife leisurely and pleasantly. He does the work mechanically. He does not take care of her psychological views for making life more pleasant, more enjoyable by going for outings, picnics, and pastime activities.

Besides all these things, his routine and tight schedule for the day-to-day administration of Satipur province has disturbed the peace of his family life. Olivia is often obsessed with the idea that Douglas has time for others and not for her. Douglas feels that his wife should be a conformist, but Olivia feels that she is not an 'object' but a human being with her own psychological and emotional desires. Though she is materially well off and has all the comforts, her emotional life is badly shattered. Douglas thinks that the closed bungalow without heat and dust, the servants to carry out the orders of his wife, food to eat, books to read and piano to play on are enough to stay at home and live happily. But Olivia thinks that there are certain situations when she needs her husband; he should sit with her without hurried programmes, talk to her without administrative worries, and move together keeping the wife and administraion separately. She feels that there must be a fixed time for administration and the rest of the time should be for her only as she wants to be the queen of her life with pleasures but not with pains with such dry life. Somehow, the conservative mind of Douglas does not suit the mental behaviour of his wife. Therefore, she diverts her mind towards the Nawab and she takes his help for the outings. During one of her secret visits to the Nawab that she pays without the knowledge and permission of her husband, she tells Harry that she does not want to see the Begum [Nawab's mother] but is interested in the Nawab. "I come here to be with you—and him of course—I mean, as your friend. Both of you" (102). She likes the Nawab Sahib very much. He is very strong. She is charmed by him. His gay and courteous manners, his mellifluous voice in reciting Urdu poetry, his luxurious palace and its inscrutable interiors, his grand parties attract Olivia. She feels that there is life in the temperament of the Nawab. As a young European girl, it is such Oriental aspects which impress her. Compared to the charming Nawab, the Anglo-Indian officials appear quite boring to Olivia. "She kept asking herself how it was possible to lead exciting lives—administering whole provinces, fighting border battles, advising rulers—and at the same time to remain so dull" (15). Thus, Douglas' absence of feelings towards the emotional feelings of Olivia creates a gulf between wife and husband. Laurie Sucher opines that this "novel is rich in nature imagery. It contrasts the heat and dust of the plains—which signify at once an obsessive sexuality and the absence of feeling—with the life-giving moisture of the Himalayas." (99)

There is another reason for Olivia's boredom. As India is not the motherland of Anglo-Indians, they are not rooted in the cultural heritage of India. The husband, Douglas, is obsessed with his job, and the wife, Olivia, gets bored in the spacious bungalow. Here love exists only at the physical level and not at the psychological level. She is a non-conformist and wants her own way of life. She does not like the traditional way of life of her husband. She has an inquisitive mind which is eager to know something about Indian culture and civilisation. For this Olivia takes the help of the Nawab. The Nawab acts as the guide and subsequently he develops friendship with Olivia. Olivia, who is disgusted with her life since she has not been blessed with a child, finds these attentions quite refreshing. As a matter of fact, the Anglo-Indians are conscious of the need of procreating a race which would inherit the ideal British qualities. Since Douglas represents such ideals and qualities, a whole lot of Douglases is needed to the people of the world. Both Douglas and Olivia are keen to have children. Time passes, but Olivia does not conceive. She herself is worried about it. Behind her worry is the assumption that the world would be poorer without the progeny of the Douglas couple dominating it. "She could not believe it; she was sure that a couple like herself and Douglas were meant to have children, to be the founders of a beautiful line. He too was sure of it" (105). Curiously, Olivia does not ascribe her supposed infertility to any biological defect or physical incompatibility. She comes out with a psychological reason which itself gives a distorted picture of the country. She says that she could not conceive because "she had been so frightened by all the little babies in the graveyard, dead of smallpox, dead of cholera, dead of enteric fever" (105). Thus the rate of child mortality is exaggerated and the country is depicted as afflicted with terrible fevers and diseases. She is so dissatisfied with her life besides these factors that she feels like Mrs. Kaul in *A Backward Place*,'a bird in a gilded cage.' It is natural that she cannot be happy in the modern world.

As a young bride, Olivia adores Douglas Rivers' gentlemanly idealism. She loves his English solidness and strength but with the passing of time and closer perspective of wifehood, her ardour fades. She suddenly thinks about him and says: "What manliness? He can't even get me pregnant!" (116) Then, she allows herself to be drawn into a liaison with a powerless minor prince of Khatm as that is the only option left to her. It is an option between a wooden British official and a charming Nawab; she prefers the latter. There was no alternative option left to her but to decide to go with the Nawab because she has become "like the lovesick ladies of the Kangra miniature paintings, who toss on their lovely embroidered couches while dust-storms gather threateningly overhead, she is racked by the delicate fire of a passion that her affectionate but unimaginative husband fails to recognise although he had seen a lot of Indian fevers."[46]

Prompted by the decision to opt for Eastern way of life, she goes to the shrine of Baba Firdous, at the invitation of the Nawab. There she sees the gang of dacoits armed with guns saluting the Nawab. She suspects their relationship with the Nawab but he clarifies that they are good people. She believes him and "he respectfully touched her arm with his finger-tips." (134). In gay mood, the Nawab also describes to her the way his ancestor, Amanulla Khan, was treated by the British people and he in a gloomy mood terms them as very cunning. He suddenly cries and gets upset. Olivia cannot tolerate his misery. So, "she put out her hand and laid it on his chest as if to soothe him. And really he was soothed; he said, 'How kind you are to me.' He laid his hand on top of hers and pressed it closer against his chest. She felt drawn to him by a strength, a magnetism that she had never yet in all her life expected with anyone" (136). Later, "he led her away from the shrine and they lay together under a tree" (137). She cannot resist the temptation to love him. In Nirmal

Mukherji's view, "Olivia is destroyed because she is the most vulnerable. She who is sensitive, passionate, human, and aesthetic is destroyed, whereas the 'tough old hens' like Mrs. Crawford and Mrs. Minnies survive."[46]

Olivia becomes pregnant. She first informs the Nawab Sahib and later her husband. Both the lover and the husband were happy over this news but Olivia worries more when she comes to know that her would-be child will have black hair on the head because she knows that the Nawab and not her husband was the father. So, she opts for an abortion under the supervision of the Nawab's mother and subsequently she is admitted to the hospital where Dr. Saunders declares that it is a case of abortion. When everything becomes public, she straightaway goes to the palace of the Nawab who in turn provides her accommodation at the Himalayas. There she breathes her last.

Olivia's tragedy is due to her marriage with Douglas without love and her love with the Nawab of Khatm without marriage. Her delusion of dissatisfaction, and emotional behaviour leads her towards a destructive sexual passion for which she is responsible. Her obsession with the romantic Eastern view makes her a tragic victim. Olivia's story, thus, sets an extreme example of marital dissonance resulting from cross-cultural contact.

## NOTES

1. Khushwant Singh, "India, The Literary Scene," *International Literary Annual*, III (London: 1961), p. 174.
2. H.M. Williams, "Strangers in a Backward Place: Modern India in the Fiction of Ruth Prawer Jhabvala," *The Journal of Commonwealth Literature*, vol. 6, No. 1 (June 1971), p. 53.
3. According to Richard Lannoy, the joint family is a microcosm of the profoundly pluralistic nature of Indian culture in all its manifestations. It is mostly patriarchal consisting of three to four generations living under one roof pooling their resources as well as their poverty and sharing the joys and sorrows together. Richard Lannoy, *The Speaking Tree* (London: Oxford University Press, 1971), p. 88.

4. R.P. Jhabvala, *The Householder* (London: John Murray, 1960; Penguin, 1980).
5. See R.C. Majumdar, ed., *The History and Culture of the Indian People*, Vol. I, *The Vedic Age* (London: George Allen & Unwin, 1951, 1957), pp. 493-94. The Brahamanans' supreme genius for compromise and adjustments of differences probably led later to the formulation of the theory of *Ashrams* or different stages of Aryan life. (1) In the forest one lives with a teacher and learns the *Veda* as a *Brahmacharin*; (2) as a householder, *Grihastha*, he next founds a household, begets children and himself offers sacrifices; (3) when grown old, he leaves his house and village for the forest where as a *Vanaprastha* (forest-hermit) he offers only minimum sacrificial services and devotes himself mainly to meditation; (4) *Sanyasin* who gives up even sacrifice, in fact, all good works, and as an ascetic, renounces the world to meditate on the Absolute *Brahman*, with a view to realising it or achieving union with it.
6. Yasmine Gooneratne, *Silence, Exile and Cunning: The Fiction of Ruth Prawer Jhabvala* (New Delhi: Orient Longman, 1983), p. 22.
7. Linda Warley, "The Cuckoo's Nest: House and Home in Two Early Novels of Ruth Prawer Jhabvala," Ralph J. Crane, ed., *Passages to Ruth Prawer Jhabvala* (Bangalore: Sterling, 1991), p. 25.
8. Ruth Prawer Jhabvala, *Get Ready for Battle* (London: John Murray, 1962; Penguin, 1981)
9. The Charvaka's theory is enumerated by Dr. S. Radhakrishnan in his book *Indian Philosophy*. Lokayatra is the name given to this materialistic theory. According to Charvaka, the sense of perception is the only form of knowledge and material is the only reality. The ultimate principles were four elements: earth, water, fire and air. "Wealth and enjoyment are the objects of human existence. Matter can think. There is no other world. Death is the end of all." Thus it stands for sensualism, selfishness and the gross affirmation of loved will. Dr. S. Radhakrishnan, *Indian Philosophy* (London: 1929), p. 279.
10. *Ibid.*, p. 281.
11. Vasant A. Shahane, *Ruth Prawer Jhabvala* (New Delhi: Arnold Heinemann, 1976), p. 106.
12. *Ibid.*, p. 102.
13. H.M. Williams, "Strangers in a Backward Place," p. 58.

14. According to the *Bhagavad Geeta*, both *Sanyasa* and *Karmayoga*—the renunciation of actions and performance of action—lead to *Moksha*, as giving rise to spiritual knowledge.
15. The term was first used by Khushwant Singh, in "India, the Literary Scene," *International Literary Annual* III (London, 1961), p. 174: "Jhabvala's . . . *nouveau rich* Babbitts (sic) of New Delhi." Haydn Moore Williams later developed this fruitful comparison of Ruth Prawer Jhabvala's money-minded characters to Sinclair Lewis's satirical exposure of American bourgeois society.
16. H.M. Williams, "The Yogi and the Babbitt: Themes and Characters of the New India in the Novels of Ruth Prawer Jhabvala," *Twentieth Century Literature*, Vol.15, No. 2 (July 1969), p. 89.
17. R.P. Jhabvala, *Esmond in India* (London: George & Unwin, 1958).
18. Shyam M. Asnani, "Jhabvala's Novels: A Thematic Study," *The Journal of Indian Writing in English*, 2: No. 1 (1974), p. 39.
19. Ramlal Agarwal, *Ruth Prawer Jhabvala: A Study of Her Fiction* (New Delhi: Sterling, 1990), p. 34.
20. H.M. Williams, "Strangers in a Backward Place," p. 62.
21. Yasmine Gooneratne, p. 114.
22. Vasant A. Shahane, *Ruth Prawer Jhabvala*, (New Delhi: Arnold-Heinemann, 1976), p. 89.
23. H.M. Williams, "The Yogi and the Babbitt," p. 87.
24. Meena Belliappa, "A Study of Her Fiction," *The Miscellancy* (Jan.-July 1971), No. 43, p. 40.
25. Laurie Sucher, *The Fiction of Ruth Prawer Jhabvala: The Politics of Passion* (London: Macmillan, 1989), p. 15.
26. Woman, according to Manu, should be protected and honoured at all stages of life. Her father should protect her in her childhood, her husband should protect her in her youth and her son should protect her in her old age. Woman should not be left unguarded. Trans. *Manudharmashastra* (Madras: Kewal Matwam, 1958), p. 110.
27. Ramlal Agarwal, "An Interview with Ruth Prawer Jhabvala," *Quest* 91 (Sept.-Oct. 1974), p. 36.
28. "A Novelist of India reflects two Worlds," *New York Times*, Tuesday 17 July, 1973; rep. "Rot and deep sense of melancholy" in the *National Times* (Australia) of 7-12 January 1974; qtd. Yasmine Gooneratne in "Contemporary India in the Writing of Ruth Prawer Jhabvala," *Westerly*, Vol. 28, No. 4 (Dec. 1983), p. 73.

29. Caroline Moorhead, "A Solitary Writer's Window on the Heat and Dust of India," *The Times* (20 November 1975), p. 16.
30. R.P. Jhabvala, *A Backward Place* (London: John Murray, 1965; Penguin, 1980).
31. R.P. Jhabvala, "Myself in India," *An Experience of India* (1971; London: John Murray, 1996), p. 7.
32. Ralph J. Crane, ed., Introduction of *Passages to Ruth Prawer Jhabvala* (Bangalore: Sterling, 1991), p. ix.
33. H.M. Williams, "Strangers in a Backward Place," p. 60.
34. R.P. Jhabvala, "Myself in India," *An Experience of India*, p. 10.
35. *Ibid.*, p. 13.
36. *Ibid.*, p. 14.
37. A. Jaganmohana Chari, "Journey into the 'That'—'There' World": A Study of Ruth Prawer Jhabvala's Novel, *A Backward Place,"* *Kakatiya Journal of English Studies*, Vol. 3, No. 1 (1978), p. 141.
38. H.M. Williams, "Strangers in a Backward Place," p. 60.
39. H.M. Williams, *The Fiction of Ruth Prawer Jhabvala* (Calcutta: Writers' Workshop, 1973), p. 49.
40. R.P. Jhabvala, *Heat and Dust*, (London: John Murray, 1975).
41. H.S. Mahle, *Indo-Anglian Fiction: Some Perceptions* (New Delhi: Jaisons, 1985), p. 28.
42. A. Ramakrishna Rao, "Complex, Racial Image in Jhabvala's *Heat and Dust*," *The Journal of English Studies*, 13, No. 2 (April 1982), p. 66.
43. K.P.K. Menon, "Parallel Plots in *Heat and Dust*, *Littcrit*, 10 No. 1 (June 1984), p. 46.
44. Ramesh Chadha, "*Heat and Dust* and *Coffer Dams*: A Comparative Study," *The Journal of Indian Writing in English*, 10: Nos. 1-2 (1982), p. 26.
45. Yasmine Gooneratne, p. 217.
46. Nirmal Mukherji, "*Heat and Dust*: A Tale of Two Women," *Kakatiya Journal of English Studies*, 3, No. 1 (1978), p. 122.

Chapter III

# A Study of Anita Desai's Novels

As a novelist, Anita Desai does not believe in propagandist writing. Writing, she says, is a process of discovery. The purpose of writing is to discover the truth and then describe and convey the truth. Desai's search for truth has resulted in portraying women characters suffering from marital dissonance. Desai has drawn her female protagonists from the middle class and upper-middle class sections of Indian urban areas. She has an independent approach to women's problems in Indian social life as well as life in general. She does not subscribe to the prevalent view of male-dominated society that a woman's body and soul are the same. Desai has a definite idea of a happy conjugal life. To her, marriage is a union and communion of two different minds. Some of her young immature, romantic heroines seem to have this definite idea of a blissful and happy conjugal life; but the idea seems to remain only a rainbow dream.

The concept of marriage which is related to a delicate union of two different minds has not been properly realized in most of the Indian male-dominated families. Woman's individual identity, her desires, her feelings, her psychological temperament have not been positively studied in Indian social life. It is very unfortunate that in India women have never been accepted as full human beings. The casual attitude of man towards woman is responsible for her consistent suffering and miserable fate. Anita Desai is concerned with the inner world of an individual. She prefers to delve "deeper and deeper in a character or a scene, rather than going round about it."[1] Desai prefers the private world to the public world. She is a painter of moods and wills of conflicting choices and experiences but not surface realities. Commenting on Anita Desai's art and technique, Ramesh K. Srivastava remarks: "She being a housewife and having selected family relationships as her two inches of ivory, Anita Desai, an Indian Jane Austen and Virginia Woolf blended, is not so much concerned with outer as with the inner weather. Unlike a photographer concerned with the portrayal of surface reality, she is a painter of moods and of wills; of conflicting choices and of inner experiences. The subjects of the novels are not poverty or riches, wars, political upheavals, social evils, but the incompatibility of marriage and inharmonious man-woman relationship."[2]

Anita Desai focuses on man in conflict with his mind. Her forte is the exploration of the human psyche. Her female characters are generally neurotics, highly sensitive, out of harmony with their husbands and circumstances. The result is marital dissonance. The psychological and temperamental reasons for the problem of marital dissonance are different from one couple to another in her novels. Commenting on the existential problems of Anita Desai's characters, Seema Jena remarks: "Each of her novels is primarily designed to project one or two memorable characters. In the character portrayal again, she is primarily interested in the projection of female protagonists living in a separate, closed, sequestered world of existential problems and passions, love and hatred; she portrays her characters as individuals facing single-handedly, the ferocious assaults of existence."[3]

The theme of marital dissonance figures quite prominently in five of Desai's novels taken up for study here. In *Cry, the Peacock* and *Voices in the City*, Anita Desai presents the theme of marital dissonance resulting from lack of love, and consequently leading to the suffering and suicide of women characters, while in *Where Shall We Go This Summer*? and *Fire on the Mountain*, her women protagonists move from alienation to adjustment and from adjustment to alienation respectively. In *In Custody*, Anita

Desai locates the problems of marital dissonance in the socio-economic factors.

### 1 From Frustration to Death: *Cry, the Peacock* and *Voices in the City*

*Cry, the Peacock*[4] is Anita Desai's first novel. This novel has been hailed by many critics as a significant achievement in the realm of Indian English fiction. Meena Belliappa considers it as "a remarkable attempt to fuse fantasy with perpetual experience"[5] while Darshan Singh Maini terms it as "a poetic novel."[6] R.S. Sharma considers it as "the first step in the direction of psychological fiction in English."[7]

Maya, the central character in the novel, is beautiful, intelligent and very sensitive as well as sensuous but she fails to grow out of childhood. She is married to Gautama who is many years senior to her. He is a successful lawyer practising in Delhi. There is apparently nothing that is common to them—social status, educational background, intellectual training, emotional make up and religious and moral outlook. Yet, they have managed to complete three years of married life. The moment she enters the fourth year of her marriage, she remembers the prophecy of an albino astrologer who in her impressionable childhood, predicted that she or her husband would die during the fourth year of their marriage. During the period of four years of her married life, she fails to establish effective communication with her husband who is detached, rational and twice her age. Her husband's indifference to her agonised predicament and her childless life heightens her sense of marital dissonance and consequently she kills her husband, Gautama, by pushing him off the parapet of their house, in a fit of insane fury.

*Cry, the Peacock* has three parts. While part I of the novel depicts the death of Maya's pet dog Toto, and records Maya's feelings towards the dead dog, part II hints at the death of the protagonist herself. Anita Desai chooses to avoid the details of the death pertaining to Maya. The last paragraph of part II delineates the death of Gautama, Maya's husband. Anita Desai transforms the neurotic problem of marital dissonance into a moving study of the psyche of Maya who wants to seek love, sympathy and understanding but suffers intensely every moment. Marital dissatisfaction, an acute feeling of isolation and an obsessive fear of death aggravate her misery and cause in her a sense of utter marital dissonance.

Maya is a spoilt and pampered daughter of Raisahib, a wealthy Brahmin of Lucknow. Gautama is the protege of Raisahib. He finds Gautama agreeable for marriage with his daughter on two counts: first he resembles himself in age and intelligence. Raisahib perhaps feels that a person of Gautama's age and understanding will give the kind of protection to Maya which he himself has been giving. Secondly, Gautama presents a complete contrast to Arjuna (Maya's brother) in his elitism and is similar to Maya in her submissiveness. Another mundane explanation is that Raisahib has to unburden himself of the responsibility of a grown-up daughter by arranging the marriage at the earliest, which is not surprising in India where a daughter is held to be a mortgage and a son a dividend. Reacting to this arrangement, Maya says, "our marriage was grounded upon the friendship of the two men, and the mutual respect in which they held each other, rather than upon anything else" (40). Their incompatible temperaments make it difficult for them to have a warm, harmonious relationship and subsequently pave the way for their estrangement. While Maya is dreamy, sensitive and emotional, Gautama is rational, insensitive and practical. Maya is poetic and instinctive, while Gautama is detached and philosophical. K.K. Sharma rightly remarks that the novel "highlights the problem of unequal marriage."[8] Gautama and Maya cannot have emotional bonds between them because of their incongruous natures. Frustrated, Maya rightly observes: "Our marriage was based upon a nobility forced upon us from outside, and therefore neither true nor lasting. It was broken repeatedly, and repeatedly the pieces were picked up and put together again" (40).

Having had a carefree life in her father's house, Maya desires to have the same in her husband's. Gautama, who is treated almost as the father-substitute by Maya, is too engrossed in his own vocational affairs to pay her the attention that she expects. He has neither the time nor the concern for showing tenderness to her. Consequently she feels isolated, neglected and miserable. The alienation results from the sharp contrast between cold detachment and warm imagination. Besides this, Maya's problem is her existential predicament, her feminine obsessions such father-fixation. Whenever she is mentally perturbed or in crisis, she recollects her life with her father who brought her up very affectionately. Such moments of nostalgia offset the rising frustration, despair and boost her drooping spirits. Maya's father had a lot of love for his daughter and gave her freedom to do whatever she liked:

> When I play battledore and shuttlecocks, using the small bright oranges as shuttlecocks that shoot, bird-like, through the air and are broken, egg like, on the grass he only laughs to see me leap and fly, leap and fly. (44)

Such a free life enjoyed by Maya turns into a life in a cage after her marriage. Maya is already obsessed with the prophecy of an albino astrologer. In her relationship with Gautama, she missed the attachment with her father. Apart from these social factors, Maya expects a measure of emotional and physical satisfaction in married lives which are denied to her, one by Gautama's cold intellectuality and the other by his age and diligence in work. The following passage demonstrates her mixed feelings towards the fact of her being his wife:

> Poor man. Poor Gautama. My husband. I spoke these words in order to stop staring, to make myself feel something for him. Gautama, my husband rose and went up to him, beginning to feel as tenderly solicitous towards him as towards a departing guest who might never be encountered again, and I strolled with him slowly across the lawn, feeling that an unreal ghost stalked beside me—a body without a heart, a heart without a body—what was he?

> An unfair question, oh, grossly unfair, I chided myself immediately. He was a tired man, worn out by a day's hard, concentrated work. Age surrounded him, weariness steeped his limbs. Grey, grey, all was grey for Gautama, who lived so narrowly, so shallowly. And I felt sorry, infinitely sorry for him, for this slow, harmless, guileless being who walked the fresh grass and did not know he touched it. (196-97)

Consequently, her longing for intimacy with Gautama leads her to the realisation that there is no bond left between them that would unite and hold them in love:

> Had there been a bond between us, he would have felt its pull, I thought of him so deeply. But, of course, there was none. That had been proved to me tonight. There was no bond, no love—hardly any love. And I could not bear to think of that. (108)

Sigmund Freud[9] views that sex is not only an intensely and intrinsically pleasurable experience but it can act as a revitalising force in an otherwise sterile life. It is the prototype of all pleasurable experiences of life. Maya's earthly nature makes her well-inclined to derive the fullest satisfaction from this intimate experience. Unfortunately, Maya is often disillusioned in sex. There are several passages in *Cry, the Peacock*, which portray Maya's dissatisfaction in sexual life. Maya frankly admits her sexual dissatisfaction born of Gautama's unpardonable negligence:

> Telling me to go to sleep while he worked at his papers, he did not give another thought to me, to either the soft, willing body or the lonely, wanting mind that waited near his bed. (9)

Gautama also does not bother to notice the inner yearnings of Maya. She says:

> I turned upon my side, closer to him, conscious of the swell of my hip that rose under the white sheet which fell in sculptured folds about my rounded form. His eyes remained blank of appraisal, of any response. It was as though he had seen only what he had expected to see, nothing less, and nothing more. (41-42)

For her unqualified love for Gautama she suffers from "a humiliating sense of neglect, of loneliness, of desperation" (201). She starts sexualising her surroundings, perhaps by way of substitution. The papaya trees in the courtyard, for example, assume a new sexual significance for her:

> I contemplated that, smiling with pleasure at the thought of those long streamers of bridal flowers that flow out of the core of the female papaya tree and twine about her slim trunk, and the firm, wax-petalled blossoms that leap directly out of the solid trunk of the male. (92)

As her grip over herself begins to slacken, she begins to experience hallucinatory visions of lizards and birds copulating in unusual settings:

> Of the lizards, the lizards that come upon you, stalking you silently, upon clawed toes, slipping their clublike tongues in and out, in and out with an audible hiss . . . they have struck you to a pillar of salt which, when it is motionless they will mount and lash with their slime-dripping tongues, lash and lash again, as they grip you with curled claws, rubbing their cold bellies upon yours, rubbing and grinding, rubbing and grinding. (127)

What Maya experiences in her fantasy seems to be a symbolic satisfaction of the sexual desire which she misses in her actual life. The image of fighting and mating peacocks, the central motif of the novel, underlines Maya's sexual frustration too. The memory of her innocent enjoyment of their call in her childhood becomes a foil to her mind now over-crowded with animal imagery:

> But sleep was rent by the frenzied cries of peacocks pacing the rocks at night—peacocks searching for mates, peacocks tearing themselves to bleeding shreds in the act of love, peacocks screaming with agony at the death of love. The night sky turned to a flurry of peacocks' tails, each star a staring eye. (175)

In spite of her total frustration, Maya does not cross the bounds of marital harmony. She is not in a position to sublimate this powerful biological urge in the manner of her friend, Leila, who serves her ailing husband. Maya's married life ends up in sterility.

Lack of fulfilment of the body's sexual needs proves disastrous to Maya who is hypersensitive in her disposition. A healthy emotional life would have given her a sense of security and stopped her psyche from further decay. Failure on this front only hastens her to seek a neurotic solution. Freud says:

> Experience shows . . . that women, who, as being the actual vehicle of the sexual interests of mankind, are only endowed in a small measure, with the gift of sublimating their instincts, and who . . . when they are subjected to the disillusionments of marriage, fall ill of severe neuroses which permanently darken their lives.[10]

Freud attributes neurosis of women to sexual dissatisfaction resulting from the rigours of civilized sexual morality. Biologically speaking, marital unfaithfulness could be a viable cure for the ailment. However, such a thing is not possible in the Indian society. Freud explains:

> The more strictly a woman has been brought up and the more sternly she has submitted to the demands of civilization, the more she is afraid of taking this way out; and in the conflict between her desires and her sense of duty, she once more seeks refuge in a neurosis. Nothing protects her virtue as securely as an illness. (47)

Maya develops a sense of longing for outdoor life for relief. As a child she had enjoyed the scenic beauty and the cool weather of Darjeeling and now she longs to go there with Gautama. When she timidly suggests the possibility to Gautama, he responds in a cold tone, "Why don't you? . . . your father would take you wherever you wanted to go. He can" (40). The Kathakali battles played at night in parts of India, hold great attraction to Maya:

> I want—I want, . . . to see the Kathakali dances. I have heard of ballets they have in their villages. . . . And the dancers are all men. . . . The masks they wear—you must have seen them? And their costumes. And the special kind of music. And it is all out in the

> open, at night, by starlight—and perhaps they have torches. (42-43)

To her imploration to take her to the South, Gautama coolly suggests that she should wait till a Kathakali troupe comes to Delhi. Gautama's pragmatism and unromantic attitude to life and callous behaviour intensifies Maya's mental suffering. Maya's preference for the romantic feelings clash with Gautama's materialistic attitude.

Maya's sense of isolation and passivity reaches such heights that she willingly welcomes even the violent and the bizarre if they can cause a stir in her stagnant life. As has been pointed out by Sudhakar Ratnakar Jamkhandi, "it becomes beyond her capacity to involve herself in some useful work against the background of long experience of neglect."[11] All that she can now do is to turn inward and contemplate upon albino's prophecy that her marriage fails in its fourth year with the death of either wife or husband. She is terribly scared of death and feels that "Torture, guilt, dread, imprisonment were the four walls of my private hell." Fear of death turns her into a brooding introvert.

The death of Toto, her pet dog, upsets Maya and creates in her an awareness of death which fills her with fear. She says:

> Something slipped into my tear-hazed vision, a shadowy something, that prodded me into admitting that it was not my pet's death alone that I mourned to-day, but another sorrow, unremembered, perhaps as yet not even experienced, and filled me with this despair. (8)

The death of Toto is a spiritual catastrophe in Maya's life. Anita Desai comments, "the death of Toto in *Cry, the Peacock*, is the symbol of death, annihilation and destruction of the vulnerable and the protected."[12] Gautama does all that is to be done quickly and quietly like a "surgeon's knife at work." Toto's death does not mean anything to him. It evokes neither sorrow nor pity in him. He is unaware of the impact of Toto's death on Maya's sensitive psyche. In a cool tone, he consoles her saying, "It is all over, come and drink your tea, and stop crying." Maya feels miserable and isolated as she fails to receive Gautama's sympathy and understanding. "His coldness, and incessant talk of cups of tea and philosophy in order not to hear me talk and, talking, reveal myself. It is that—my loneliness in this house" (9). Maya feels lonely, neglected and blames her husband for it. Maya's subjectivity and attachment is in sharp contrast to Gautama's objectivity and detachment. Shanta Acharya aptly observes: "Maya and Gautama end up being two sides of the same coin; in each case the exclusiveness of the self makes it unable to accommodate the other."[13] The irreconcilable temperaments of Gautama and Maya result in the lack of communication between them creating marital dissonance.

Maya develops a sense of depression due to the indifference of Gautama. She remembers the peacock's dance. During the dance, the peacock's cry "Lover, Lover. Mio, Mio, I die" symbolically suggests the "heroine's love of life and obsession with death which leads her to the final crack up."[14] R.S. Sharma also observes that "the cry of the peacock is symbolic of Maya's life-in-death and death-in-life." (25) Maya's life, like the peacock's dance of joy, also implies death. It is believed that at the sight of monsoon clouds, the peacocks cry for their lovers and death. While dying they show their longing and love for life. So, "living, they are aware of death. Dying they are in love with life." The astrologer's prediction places Maya in an analogous situation. She is painfully aware of death while being alive. Maya's marital dissonance is symbolized in the peacocks' fighting before mating. Maya feels that the agony of the peacock is her own. Thinking of the prediction of the astrologer she becomes disturbed:

> God, now I was caught in the net of the inescapable, and where lay the possibility of mercy, of release? This net was no hallucination, no. In the daytime, amidst companions, I could force myself into believing that it was only a nightmare, no more. But, in the night, under the stark gaze of the moon, in that waiting silence, my memories came to life, were so vivid, so detailed, I knew them to be real, too real. Or is it madness? Am I gone insane? Father!

> Brother! Husband! Who is my saviour? I am in need of one. I am dying, and I am in love with living. I am in love, and I am dying. (97-98)

Thus Maya expresses the agony caused by the haunting nightmare of death.

The extreme and irreparable situations in the married life of Maya and Gautama take them towards a philosophy of detachment but not without variance in their concepts. Maya reads *slokas* from *the Geeta*[15] and understands detachment differently. "He is fit to attain immortality who is serene and not affected by these sensations, but is the same in pleasure and pain" (108). In Maya's view one can attain immortality if one keeps one's senses under control by discipline and be a *Sthitapragna*. She reads another *sloka* from *the Geeta*, "He whose mind is not agitated in calamities and who has no longing for pleasure, free from attachment, fear and anger, he indeed is said to be a steady wisdom" (109). For Maya detachment is an essential concomitant of life and action. But for Gautama, detachment is an abstraction totally unrelated to his life. He is neither capable of attachment nor detachment. He seems to mistake indifference for non-attachment. He too quotes from the *Geeta*:

> Thinking of sense objects, man becomes attached thereto. From attachment arises longing and from longing anger is born. From anger arises delusion; from delusion, loss of memory is caused. From loss of memory discriminative faculty is ruined and from the ruin of discrimination, he perishes. (112)

By quoting this he emphasizes detachment but it is a dry, mechanical kind of detachment with something inhuman about it. So Maya describes him as an "inhuman dry stick."

Gautama traces Karma theory more to logic than to faith. He believes that action is more important than inaction in life. He also believes that those who have a vocation can attain peace and serenity. His understanding of the *Geeta* is mechanical. His detachment which almost borders on inhumanity becomes a curse to Maya. Maya compares her position to that of the caged monkeys. She gazes at the caged monkeys with tears in her eyes: "Some clung to the rails, staring out with glazed eyes of tragedy, at the horrible vision of hell before them, close and warm and stifling" (154).

Maya's predicament is worsened by the dust storm. The storm outside is symbolic of the rising storm in her mind. The dust storm is a physical manifestation of the struggle between life and death in the private world of Maya's soul. It is also the symbol of her release and liberation from her miserable predicament. Gautama is moved neither by the storm nor by her suffering. He is content with a cup of tea and a cold shower and some rest. When Gautama fails to notice the storm, Maya feels that her unexpressed decision to get rid of her husband is right. She thinks that she is committed to life, whereas Gautama is detached and indifferent. She thinks: "the man had no contact with the world or with me. What would it matter to him if he died or lost" (175). Maya thinks her life instinct is thwarted by his indifference and so she decides to kill him.

At several places in the novel, Desai hints at Maya's celebration of instinctual life by showing her keen aesthetic interest in nature. It is the life of instincts which takes one close to nature and strengthens the kinship with it. In the novel, Maya represents the world of instincts whereas Gautama represents the world of intellect. Thus they remain like two parallel lines which never meet. In the following passage, which is poetic and ritualistic, she wants to merge with the elements of nature, but finds Gautama a disgusting hurdle with his stress on intellect, standing rocklike between her and the elements of nature. Therefore, she eliminates this hurdle by throwing him down the terrace:

> I saw the moon's vast, pure surface, touched only faintly with petals of shadow, as though brushed by a luna moth's wings, so that it appeared a great multifoliate rose, waxen white, virginal, chaste and absolute white casting a light that was holy in its purity, a soft, suffusing glow of its chastity, casting its reflection upon the night with a vast, tender mother love.

> And then Gautama made a mistake—his last, decisive one. In talking, gesturing, he moved in front of me, thus coming between me and the worshipped moon, his figure an ugly, crooked grey shadow that transgressed its sorrowing chastity. 'Gautama,' I screamed in fury, and thrust out my arms towards him, out at him, into him and past him, saw him fall then, pass through an immensity of air, down to the very bottom. (208)

With the death of Gautama, Maya's marital dissonance reaches the climax.

Realities which are not immediately perceptible are reflected in the novels of Anita Desai. In *Cry, the Peacock*, she goes deep into the sources of marital dissonance in a male-dominated society. She depicts with great sensitivity the dissolution of feminine sensibility under the stress of marriage that finally destroys Maya herself. Maya's external world of society, her frustrated life with Gautama, friends and the inner world with her perceptions and physical needs are in conflict. Therefore, the barrier between the two worlds is broken with the killing of Gautama. Maya seeks her redemption in the killing of Gautama which turns her life into a tragedy. This tragedy could have been averted had she received some sympathy and understanding from Gautama. The novel concludes with the suggestion of the suicide of Maya. The details of Maya's death are not given in the novel but the 'screaming' of Maya could be heard while "there was silence, and then both disappeared into the dark quiet. All around the dark was quiet then" (218).

The death of Gautama is the end of the story but not the end of the problem for Maya. The agony and frustration experienced by Maya due to marital dissonance finds its logical end in her own tragic suicide. The impact of marital dissonance is greater on Maya than on Gautama.

In her second novel, *Voices in the City*[16] (1965), Anita Desai presents the most pathetic illustration of maladjustment in marriage. The tragedy of extreme sensitiveness and the resultant marital dissonance which are dealt with in Desai's first novel, *Cry, the Peacock*, are also continued in *Voices in the City*. This novel deals with the situations of Monisha's boredom, her husband Jiban's non-cooperation, in their lack of privacy, domination of the mother-in-law and the absurdity of contemporary metropolitan life in India.

Anita Desai's *Voices in the City* marks a complete departure from the exuberant lyricism and aesthetic feeling of her *Cry, the Peacock*. A.V. Krishna Rao comments: "Desai's second novel *Voices in the City*, is a complex structure of symbols and stereotypes. It is also at the same time a realistic representation of a decadent city culture whose only influence on the young adolescent minds seems to be negative, if not nihilistic."[17] Meena Belliappa remarks: "An attempt is made perhaps for the first time in Indian fiction to relate the subjective world of the individual to the spirit of the locale. The effort is to project place not only as milieu, but as a face wielding influence on the emotional being of men." (26) H M Williams opines: "There is desolation in Desai's novel, *Voices in the City*, made bearable by the brilliant, sensitive prose with which she delineates the spiritual odyssey of three young Indians in a contemporary 'city of death' Calcutta."[18]

Structurally, the novel is divided into four parts and each is named after one of the characters: 1) Nirode 2) Monisha 3) Amla and 4) Mother. Unlike Desai's other novels, this novel has three

acters who are brought to the monster city, Calcutta, feel tortured and vexed by their hollow and meaningless existence. They feel themselves caught in the clutches of the morbid city of which they are afraid. They find themselves trapped in it with no hope of escape. They are all afraid of brutal noises and the suffocating population of the city. All of them are alienated from society as well as from their widowed mother who is in love with Major Chadha. Nirode, alienated from society and from his mother, becomes rootless. He loses faith in life and develops an attitude of complete negation. He is obsessed by the desire of failure. He thinks success in anything is a spiritual failure. The freedom, knowledge and truth he seeks, are undefined and remote. Doing a meaningless and mechanical job, Nirode drifts from one person to another in the newspaper industry and experiences an emptiness, meaninglessness and alienation in life.

Nirode's sister, Monisha, is suffocated by the overpopulation of Calcutta. She is unable to find a suitable and lonely place of refuge in it. She also suffers from marital disharmony and commits suicide. Amla, Nirode's younger sister and a commercial artist, has an affair with an artist, Dharma, a married man but deserts him later as he disowns her and her daughter. At the close of each section, each of the protagonists arrives at the same realization that existence in the world is empty and a waste. Monisha takes the extreme step of burning herself to death due to her domestic dissatisfaction.

Desai presents a heart-rending account of Monisha's tragic life which has been shattered. Monisha's unbearable and tortured mentality is also shown as emptiness within as well as without. It arouses a feeling of pity, sympathy and tenderness of the miserably empty married life of Monisha. Like Maya in *Cry, the Peacock*, Monisha is married to an elderly man, Jiban, who is quite well off, but Monisha's relationship with him is clearly demarcated "only by loneliness" and lack of communication. Her father knows that Jiban and her family are completely unsuitable to Monisha's tastes and inclinations. Her father also knows that she is morbid by nature and so he arranges her marriage with Jiban, hoping to cure her morbidity. Amla wonders why Monisha has been married to Jiban who is a "boring non-entity, this blind moralist, this complacent quoter of Edmund Burke and Wordsworth, Mahatma Gandhi and Tagore, this rotund, minute-minded and limited official" (198). Monisha finds nothing in common with him and his self-centred and self-complacent family. She is estranged from Jiban as he is "the prisoner of a conventional culture in which woman's most important roles are, besides childbearing, 'cooking, cutting vegetables, serving food and brushing small children's hair' under the authority of a stern mother-in-law in a many headed family."[19] In addition to the suffering at the hands of her husband, she is asked to massage her mother-in-law's legs:

> I am summoned to massage her legs, for the aunts are all worn out. I go and massage them. It is not difficult at all. My heart stays perfectly quiet, enclosed in a sheath of such darkness as none of them would ever dare to touch. And as I massage, I do not tell myself: She is Jiban's mother, her legs give her pain, I am helping to relieve it because she is Jiban's mother and old. I tell myself: She thinks I am touching her. She thinks I am touching her feet. But I am not. I do not touch her, nor does she touch me—there is this darkness in between. They will never reach through it to me. (139)

Though Monisha serves her mother-in-law, there is a sense of alienation between them.

Despite Monisha's sincere attempts to appease the in-laws, she fails to get any sympathy and understanding from them, with the result, she feels humiliated and frustrated. Her childlessness and the ridiculous comments of her in-laws accentuate her agony:

> The womb may be in the wrong position, then also an operation is required. But it is the tubes, they are blocked. (113)

She questions:

> Is this what life is then, my life? Only a conundrum that I shall brood over forever with passion and pain, never to arrive at a solution? Only a conundrum—is that, then life? (124-25)

Monisha does not receive proper treatment from her husband also. He fails to provide basic things to her. She expects her husband to be considerate, understanding and show the tender feelings of love for her. The thirst for love in Monisha remains unfulfilled. She craves for privacy and freedom which she never gets in her life. It is a very minute thing, but when it is not fulfilled, it becomes a major issue. She feels that the joint family system in her husband's house is a great threat to her. As her relationship with her husband is devoid of love and joy, her body goes on withering and shrinking every day. She says:

> Only I wish I were given some tasks I could do alone, in privacy, away from the aunts and uncles, the cousins and nieces and nephews. Alone, I could work better, and I should feel more—whole. (115)

Monisha with her sensitive nature and her educational background does not fit in with the role of an eldest daughter-in-law of a traditional joint family. She is a bookworm and wants to be left alone to spend her time reading. But she is always imprisoned in the clutches of household slavery. Once Monisha takes some money from her husband's purse in order to clear the medical bills incurred towards her brother Nirode's treatment. This matter comes to the notice of her mother-in-law who in turn rebukes her as a thief.

> I will not have a thief in my house. . . . After all, you were the only person who was in the room all day. (137)

Despite her pleas that she took the money only for her brother's medical bill, her husband also doubts her and asks: "Why didn't you tell me before you took it?" (138). She is very upset and feels that she is lonely in the world with nobody to come to her rescue.

> I find that I am alone here. I find on this level that solitude that becomes me most naturally. I am willing to accept this status then, and to live here, a little beyond and below everyone else, in exile. (136)

Monisha often feels that her efforts to seek her identity are threatened by her husband and in-laws. She realises agonisingly that her in-laws

> put me away in a steel container, a thick glass cubicle, and I have lived in it all my life, without a touch of love or hate or warmth on me. I am locked apart from all of them, they cannot touch me, they can lip-read and misinterpret. Similarly, I cannot really hear them, I cannot understand what they say. I have never touched anyone,

> never left the imprint of my fingers on anyone's shoulders, of my tongue on anyone's damp palate.
>
> What a waste, what a waste it has been, this life enclosed in a locked container, merely as an observer, and so imperfect, so handicapped an observer at that. (239-40)

Having failed to win either the affection of her mother-in-law or the companionship of her husband, Monisha confides her feelings in Nirode. Nirode asks her to leave her husband and start living independently. But Monisha is not for it. She is thus caught in an irreconcilable situation.

Monisha finds her husband's home and the city atmosphere monotonous and stifling and yearns for the free air of Kalimpong of Darjeeling, because "the solitude of the jungles there, the aqueous shadows of the bamboo groves and the earth laid with great fallen leaves" (116) give her a sense of relief from the oppression of the joint family. Solitude, silence, privacy, space for meditation are lost to her in Calcutta. In a fit of depression and self-pity, she laments over the pathetic condition of Bengali women.

> I think of generations of Bengali women hidden behind the barred windows of half-dark rooms, spending centuries in washing clothes, kneading dough and murmuring aloud verses from the *Bhagvad Geeta* and the *Ramayana*, in the dim light of sooty lamps. (120)

She does not have the courage to rebel against such a tyrannical system nor does she have religious faith which would save her from the abyss of despair. Monisha's dilemma is whether to accept the meaningless and aimless life or revolt against it. She does not have faith in a life of compromise. Her morbid fear of confined places, her oppressive lack of privacy, her inability to bear a child, the total lack of communication with her disinterested husband, the absence of love in her life, and the resultant tormenting loneliness within, the suspicion of her in-laws who despise her as a thief—all these terribly torture her mentally and develop in her the feelings of "self-hate," which ultimately turn "into self-destruction."[20]

Monisha ultimately decides to end her life in a gruesome manner by setting herself on fire as if to seek release from the burden of life:

> The bathroom door stood open, silently but preparedly inviting. She went in and put down the container. . . . She lifted it as high as she could, with some effort for it was heavy. . . . Her body was braced against its fire, but it was barely warm, and soothing, a bath of oil . . . pungent odour of kerosene. When her blouse and sari were soaked, she lowered the tin. . . . To her astonishment, the very first match struck fire, and its clear flame was as straight and golden as a promise kept. . . . The oil soaking her garments responded with a leap of recognition . . . there, all over . . . she screamed. . . . Fell unconscious. Very quickly fell unconscious. (241-42)

The charred and mutilated body of Monisha shocks her brother, Nirode and her sister, Amla and puts Jiban and his mother to shame. Later on, Jiban gently covers the charred body and begs for forgiveness from her relatives. Her death at last severs the bonds that mutilated her soul and body in life and she is "taken away, unaccompanied by them in peace" (247).

Anita Desai's protagonists in this novel are not bogged down by routine problems of existence. Nirode is exposed to a life of semi-starvation, not for want of money but his strong desire and determination to preserve his individual identity. Monisha is married into a middle-class family not exposed to the struggle for existence. Their problems are extraordinary and subjective tormenting and exhausting. Suffering makes them aware of the reality of life. They undertake the tortuous journey of the soul. They proceed undaunted through doubt, frustration, dejection and disillusionment. Their solutions are achieved individually according to their convictions, attitudes and perspectives. It is left to them to choose acceptance or rejection, self-surrender or self-annihilation or bold rebellion. Monisha takes the extreme step of committing suicide. Nirode decides to move from profession to profession and from place to place as an act meaningful in itself. Amla's love for Dharma, the painter, rescues her from anxiety and loneliness but later on she also feels the inherent infection of Calcutta city. Only Monisha's death caused by her marital dissonance disturbs us. Her death has left a painful effect on the other characters as well in the novel.

The maladjustment in marriage between Monisha and Jiban is due to the settlement of their marriage by their parents without considering their attitudes, feelings and outlooks. The hostility of her in-laws and the social conditions are equally responsible for the marital dissonance of Monisha and Jiban. Anita Desai seems to suggest that at best marriage is a farce, at worst it is a malignancy that destroys body and soul completely.

### 2 From Self-Alienation to Self-Adjustment: *Where Shall We Go This Summer?*

Anita Desai's fictional outlook seems to have undergone a significant transformation with her novel *Where Shall We Go This Summer?*[21] Her preoccupation with the fascinating vistas of the diseased psyche of hypersensitive individuals is not so much altered. But whereas in her earlier novels, characters caught in the maze of life's problems committed suicide or sought some such melodramatic solution, the heroine of *Where Shall We Go This Summer?*, after moving dangerously off the course of the well-established and generally accepted path of life, returns to it in time to make up for the leeway. In an interview given to Atma Ram, Anita Desai makes it clear that suicide would have been "too melodramatic an alternative" for the middle-aged woman that the heroine is.[22]

The novel depicts the tension between a sensitive wife, Sita, and the rational, practical and worldly husband, Raman. The story centres round husband-wife discord, inadequacy of their mutual relationship and the resulting disaffection in marriage. The natural flow of affection between Sita and Raman is at times intact but more frequently it is blocked due to misunderstanding, lack of adequate forbearance and patience. The disaffection proceeds primarily from their temperaments. Like Gautama in *Cry, the Peacock*, Raman in *Where Shall We Go This Summer?* is a successful businessman with a pragmatic view of life. Sita is oversensitive, keen-eyed, poetic and imaginative, having more than ordinary sense. If Raman is sociable and extrovert, Sita is introvert. If Raman thinks only of the immediate present, Sita is foresighted and has higher notions about life than the average woman has. Because of such temperamental differences, their relationship is rendered discordant.

Sita has four children and is reluctant to deliver or to abort the fifth one. She wants to retain it in her womb because she is afraid of exposing the child to the violence in the modern world by giving birth. Fed up with the dreary metropolitan life in Bombay and tormented by the paranoiac fear of her fifth and reluctant pregnancy, she goes to the magic island, Manori, in the hope of preventing the delivery with the help of miracles. Having failed in her attempt, she becomes alienated. She returns home to continue her passive life. T.S. Anand aptly accounts for her return:

> She [Sita] had realised the difference between the necessity and the wish, between what a man wants and what he is compelled to do. Her desire to bear the child and return with Raman to the main land signifies her return to life, community and society in spite of the debased dullness of life, the calamity, the lies and moral buggery, the odium, the detritus of wrong and sorrow dropped on every heart, for existence is not possible in an insulted stage of being, rather existence implies being with others.[23]

The story of the novel is told in a series of flashbacks with a clever ordering of past events. The first section is devoted to Sita's coming to the "Magic Island" Manori along with her daughter Menaka and son Karan. The second part deals with Sita's life at Manori for twenty years before her second visit to the islet. The third part is about her choice of the future course. Desai adopts the pattern of monsoon to convey the tumult in Sita's mind. In her interview with Atma Ram, Desai says, "I wanted the book to follow the pattern of monsoon together darkly and threateningly to pour down wildly and passionately and then withdraw quietly and calmly."[24] This enables her to delineate the inner life of her heroine who is the central figure in the novel.

Sita is the daughter of a well-known freedom fighter who is looked upon by his disciples as "the second Gandhi." As most of her father's life was spent in jail and she had no mother to look after her, she was denied the life of a normal child. She was required to spend days on end away from home, at different places. There was no schooling to discipline her, nor was her father free to educate her in a systematic manner. Her sense of belonging was extremely tenuous:

> She belonged, if to anyone, to this whole society that existed at that particular point in history—like a lamb does to its flock and saw no reason why she should belong to one family alone. (85)

After independence, Sita's father selected Manori, a small island, to settle. He was accompanied by his disciples and his family. He called his house "Jeevan Ashram"—"The Home of Soul." It was on this island that he tried to put his social theories into practice. Many social welfare activities were undertaken by him, including digging of a well for the villagers. He offered suggestions to the villagers in regard to agriculture. Many strange things happened on the island. He used to cure the people stung by scorpion. Childless people also approached him for children. In a short time he became a legend. His *chelas*, who also used to take care of his daughter, Sita, "called him a saint, his critics a charlatan, the villagers a wizard and each produced evidence to prove his theory" (75). Sita also used to spend her time in the company of her brother, Jeevan and sister, Rekha. In course of time, her father's admirers grew large in number lured by his miracles. To Sita, her father remained an enigma. She formed uncertain and vague impressions about him. It was a mystery to Sita whether her father cured people by magic or by medicines. She was told by her brother that her mother had left for Benaras leaving the family. She feels "she came into this world motherless." Her mother's figure haunts her life and turns her into a wanderer. All these experiences develop in her an uncertain and unrealistic attitude towards life. She does not understand why her mother left her husband who was said to be a second Gandhi. After her father's death, she is brought to Bombay by Raman, the son of her father's old friend, Deedar. Raman arranges the funeral ceremony of her father. He admits her in a college. Impressed by her beauty, he marries her later "out of pity, out of lust, out of sudden will for adventure, and because it was inevitable" (99).

Raman is a businessman with good public relations. He is busy with his vocational affairs and spares little time for her. He represents pragmatism and materialistic values of the society. He has his own ways of life. He finds his activities more charming and fulfilling than his relations with his wife. He wants to exercise his full authority and control over her. His wife finds her life dull, ordinary, uninteresting and monotonous. She had anticipated Raman to be a loving husband, one who would make her realise how valuable she is to him. Raman, however, does not honour the claims of her bargain, and the dream is never realised. Raman drifts his energies towards his business and behaves like an escapist from his personal conflicts. By nature, he is not quarrelsome; he is a perfectionist. He has his own morals and standards and wants to stick to them. As a consequence, Sita and her husband begin to move apart. The difference in their personalities and tastes is so deep that even on a trifle like the visit of guests they disagree with each other. While it is a pleasure for Raman, it is painful for Sita.

Sita opines that marriage turns into a farce in the absence of love. She feels very unhappy with her husband and the in-laws. She considers life in Bombay disgusting and painful. She realises that people in cities live dull, artificial, bored, spiritually dissipated and absurd lives. She feels:

> a frog out of water in her father-in-law's "age-rotten flat" where they all live like pariahs "a life of sub-human placidity, calmness,

> and sluggishness" disinclined to introspection and introversion. She regards their soulless existence as a menace to her own marital and conjugal identity and boldly floats the dehumanising and de-stabilising norms and values of a society whose strangle hold it is difficult to escape.[25]

The people of Bombay are "nothing—nothing but appetite and sex. Only food, sex and money matter. Animals" (47).

Looking at the tender caressing of a Muslim woman by her old husband in the "Hanging Gardens," Sita feels the absence of such tender and gentle moments in her life. Her life, in contrast, looks like a "shadow, absolutely flat, uncoloured." She feels that life without love is meaningless. She says, "Their lives seemed to have one—if not meaning, then a secret, a strange, divine secret" (148). Raman does not understand the "divine secret," but at the same time he wonders how "your happiest memory is not of your children or your home but of strangers, seen for a moment, some lovers in the park" (147).

Fairly early in the novel, Sita's encounter with a foreign tourist during her tour to Ajanta and Ellora appears to be meaningful. "He seemed to be brave," she observes when Raman asks her why she has once more brought up the subject of the hitch-hiking foreigner. For Raman, he is a fool as "he did not even know which side of the road to wait on." But Sita identifies herself with him. Like him, she is also a person seeking an adventurous life. She too wants to wander like the stranger without the knowledge of the route. This shows her romantic vision of life and her immense interest in unfettered life.

Sita is estranged from her husband and children because of her emotional reactions to the incidents that occur to her in the society. She does not like violence of any kind whether in nature, society or in personal life. To her disgust, she finds it pervasive. In the novel, Desai depicts the gulf between Sita and her family in the episode of the eagle and the crows with an emphasis on Sita's sensitivity to violence. The ruthless attack of crows on the eagle is a terrible sight which sears her mind. She is shocked by the sight of the dead eagle like Maya in *Cry, the Peacock* is shocked by the sight of her dead pet dog. The situation objectifies for Sita the conflict in her own life. She identifies herself with the dead eagle. She is helpless like the eagle, in a society which is full of violence and destruction. None comes forward to protect the eagle. Her husband, Raman views this situation in a different way. He is not worried about it. Raman's sadistic delight in Sita's failure to protect the eagle intensifies her agony. Her husband and the children do not understand her problems due to the communication gap between them caused by their failure to share her attitudes and her fears and concerns. They are quite indifferent to her predicament. This trivial incident creates a gulf separating Sita from her husband and the children.

Another incident that describes the fight of *ayas* in the street brings out Sita's repulsion to violence. Karan, Sita's young son, is sent with the *ayah* to play with the other children of the neighbourhood. While the children are busy in their play, the ayas are immersed in gossip about their lovers and *memsahibs*. But within a short time Sita finds the *ayas* quarrelling, exchanging blows and saris ripping in the street. Suddenly, Sita comes out of the house, pulls out her son, and warns her *aya* Rosie to come out of the fray. She reflects: "It is like living in the wilds," she says to her husband at night: "One may be attacked—one's children may be attacked in the streets" (43-44). Sita thinks that there is no security to anyone in this violent society, a fact which she cannot tolerate, and sobs helplessly. Raman who is practical and insensitive to such happenings, takes it easy and asks Sita to close the topic because their son would be upset by it.

Once Menaka unconsciously crumbles a sheaf of new buds on the small potted plant telling her mother about a party. Sita is hurt by the sight of her daughter's insensitivity and callousness. Sita reflects:

> She [Menaka] had done it unconsciously, had not meant to destroy anything at all. Destruction came so naturally; that was horror. Even the smallest, Karan, appeared to build a tower of blocks only

> for the pure, lustful joy of throwing it over with a great clatter, so much more enjoying the downfall than the architecture. She winced and shrank, hearing those blocks crash. The creative impulse had no chance, against the overpowering desire to destroy. (45-46)

Again in another incident, Sita dislikes her husband's indifference towards the newspaper pictures of Vietnam war, the photo of a woman weeping over a grave, a crowd outside the Rhodesian jail. Menaka's tearing Sunday water colours into "long strips of meaningless colour," Karan's demolishing his toys with karate blows, articles about the perfidy of Pakistan are like "hand-grenades hurled at her frail gold fish-bowl belly." Instinctively, she lays her hands over her belly feeling:

> child there play like some soft-fleshed fish in a bowl of warm sea-water. She folded her hands over it, frightened, certain now that civilization had been created by the godlike efforts of the few, in the face of a constant, timeless war of destruction that had begun with time and was now roaring around her, battering her and her fish-foetus so that survival seemed hopeless. How could civilization survive, how could the child? How could she hold them whole and pure and unimpeached in the midst of this bloodshed? They would surely be wounded, fall and die. (55-56)

Sita becomes hysterical like Maya of *Cry, the Peacock*, and starts tossing clothes, smoking cigarettes and hurling books. Raman is baffled to notice this emotional upheaval. Even though she is forty, she has no control over herself. Sita's becoming pregnant at this age is looked at with distaste by Raman. As days pass by, the very atmosphere of Bombay becomes suffocating and insufferable for her. Her thorough disappointment and disillusionment with married life aggravates her compulsion to repeat hysterical behaviour. Her necessity assumes such a dramatic dimension as her irrational flight to the island ostensibly to prevent the birth of her child into the violence-ridden world. But actually it is a narcissistic desire to relieve the sensation of 'greatness' which was denied her in her childhood. While the Hanging Gardens episode clearly points out her neurotic need for the tender attention of her husband, the pregnancy provides an ideal occasion to think of the magic island as a source of release from the unpleasant life in Bombay. "She saw that island illusion as a refuge, a protection. It would hold her baby safely unborn, by magic" (101). So, when Raman casually asks, "Where Shall We Go This Summer?" she almost spontaneously suggests that they should go to Manori, her father's island. Sita also wants to escape to the island because:

> Her desire to abandon the sweat and turmoil of the urban atmosphere in Bombay where she and her husband Raman live with their four children in a bourgeois neighbourhood is triggered by the subtle incompatibility between husband and wife. Ironically, Raman and Sita are no mythological stereotypes. Sita, especially has left the tradition of her namesake far behind and has taken to smoking and neurotic outbursts as a result of this growing incompatibility.[26]

Sita shifts to Manori island along with her daughter Menaka and son Karan, leaving the other members of the family in Bombay, but to her surprise the magic and the special charm that once belonged to the island are no more to be found. She is disappointed with the islanders. Sita's escape to Manori is "an attempt to capture the care-free days of her childhood where time stood still and yet it was no paradise. Corruption, selfishness, egoism have all had their place there."[27] Sita finds the road, the bullock cart, the fields and the men and the women of the island, all revealing the ravages of time. The fields are only "pits of mud and slush." The old house is full of dust and cobwebs. Her old servant Moses and his wife Miriam have become lazy. Her children Menaka and Karan are reluctant to continue their stay on the island. Sita is also disappointed with this atmosphere on the island and soon she realises her folly. She admits, "It was no place in which to give birth. There was no magic here—the magic was gone" (112). She feels that her vulnerable self is attacked by alienation. She thinks that her life is meaningless and shapeless and laments for having wasted it by not giving it a direction and meaning. She reflects:

> I should have known how to channel my thoughts and feelings, how to put them to use. I should have given my life some shape then, some meaning. At least, it would have had some for me—even if no one else had cared. (117)

Sita, walking on a shell-scattered sandbar with the children, sees a dead jellyfish. The fish appears as though it is the opaque "mind" of a huge undersea creature which, after its skull has burst open, floated to the shore and stranded there. Sita is suddenly struck by the realisation that she and the foetus inside her womb are very much similar to the undersea creature and the jellyfish. Like the creature which lives "far beneath the level where light penetrated" (124) she has lived so far refusing to see the light of the realities of life. The law of nature which applied to the jellyfish will apply with equal force to her baby too. She cannot rewrite nature's law to prevent its birth.

While Sita is passing through such stupendous crises in life, Raman visits Manori island to take her back home. She finds him now agreeable for all that he does for the family. Moreover, her life at Manori island restores her to the world of hard facts and awakens her to the truth of her situation. In its very failure to offer the magic of the earlier era it provides her an ideal setting to fight her affliction—by repeating painful experience and thus gaining mastery over the situation. Sita's final decision to follow Raman to Bombay is the turning point in her mental journey which she takes in the spirit of D.H. Lawrence's verse:

> The wild young heifer, glancing distraught,
> With a strange, new knocking of life at her side
> Runs seeking a loneliness.
> The little grain draws down the earth, to hide.
> Nay, even the slumbrous egg as it labours under the shell
> Patiently to divide and sub-divide,
> Asks to be hidden, and wishes nothing to tell. (150)

Sita finds the answer to her problems in the verse. So far she has considered giving birth as an act of violence but now she realises "a seed fallen from the tree of life into the cosmic womb, must break open. Bursting out of the enclosure of the womb is a violent activity, but in its impetuosity it is creative."[28] Therefore, betrayed, realised and humiliated, Sita is forced to come back to Bombay. According to Kunj Bala Goel, "it is a state of disheartening helplessness and due to a wish to compromise with her husband."[29] Since there is no alternative, she passively affirms life. She is compelled to welcome the child into the world of violence and suffering. On being asked about the fate of the fifth child, Anita Desai in her interview with Atma Ram, answers:

> It is born. It lives. It compromises. It accepts the dullness, either closes its eyes to or else condones destruction, ugliness, rottenness. In other words, it leads an ordinary life of the kind its mother tried so desperately to change only to find she could not.[30]

Thus her return to Bombay brings her a new child safely. Menaka's admission to medical college is gained and the children are reared. And also her return to Bombay is a symbolic re-enactment of the scene twenty years ago when she followed Raman pitying herself for her helplessness; but this time it is of her own free will that she follows him like a "freed sea-bird at evening" (150), implicitly agreeing with her husband's philosophy that one should "be grateful if life is only a matter of disappointment, not disaster" (143).

Normally Desai's heroines act violently, but here is a positive change. Sita reconciles herself to her lot. She ultimately strikes a balance between her inner self and the outer world, her prosaic self and her poetic sensibility, her individual self and the social consciousness. *Where Shall We Go This Summer?* offers a contrast to the other novels like *Cry, the Peacock*, *Voices in the City* and *Fire on the Mountain*, in which the problem of marital dissonance has violent and tragic end. This novel presents a positive approach to the existential predicament. Sita simply compromises with her destiny.

## 3 From Self-Adjustment to Self-Alienation: *Fire on the Mountain*

*Fire on the Mountain,*[31] published in 1977, is Anita Desai's fifth novel and it won for her the coveted Sahitya Akademi Award for 1978. Here she explores the problem of disintegration of family life. Desai also deals here with the problem of loneliness and the resultant anguish in the marital life of Nanda Kaul. Nanda leads a life of deprivation, of unfulfilment in the house of Vice-Chancellor Kaul, teeming with plenty except true love. She leads a life without love from her husband. She lacks the marital harmony which every married woman expects from her spouse.

In *Fire on the Mountain*, Desai skilfully investigates the "emotional world" of Nanda Kaul with a rare poignancy. The problem of the husband-wife alienation once again forms the central nucleus in this novel. These three novels, according to Atma Ram, "portray female protagonists who are not average but have retreated or have been driven into some extremity of despair and so are turned against or are made to stand against, the general current."[32] By a general critical consensus, this novel is considered Desai's best because "it reveals Desai's greater control over style and matter. It is the most successful of her novels, stylistically. There is a greater sensitivity and restraint in the portrayal of a theme that is recurring in all four of her novels."[33] Anita Desai herself said: "It gave me something closest to satisfaction in which I had come closest to what I set out to do and I don't think I very often do, is *Fire on the Mountain*."[34]

The novel is divided into three parts—Part I is exclusively devoted to "Nanda Kaul at Carignano." Part II pertains to the arrival of her great granddaughter: "Raka comes to Carignano," and part III is about Nanda Kaul's friend, "Ila Das leaves Carignano."

Nanda Kaul has already discharged her duties and fulfilled all her promises, being a mother of many children. As the respectable wife of the Vice-Chancellor of Punjab University, she leads a busy life engrossed in her domestic affairs ordering "too many servants" and looking, watching and attending to many children and serving her husband efficiently:

> Too many trays of tea would have to be made and carried to her husband's study, to her mother-in-law's bedroom, to the verandah that was the gathering place for all, at all times of the day. Too many meals, too many dishes on the table, too much to wash up after. (29)

She is busily engaged in household activities and hardly gets any respite from the routine. She becomes well known for her hospitality. Her guests always remember the sophisticated Nanda Kaul in silks and pearls. Despite her busy domestic life, she gets disgusted. She feels lonely in the crowded house when her husband plays tennis with a woman, Miss David, and returns home after dropping her home. She feels suffocated in the stifling atmosphere of the house like Monisha of *Voices in the City*. As a matter of fact, she feels:

> The old house, the full house, of that period of her life when she was the Vice-Chancellor's wife and at the hub of a small but intense and busy world, had not pleased her. Its crowding had stifled her. (29)

Mrs. Nanda Kaul is tired of a long life of tedious routine. She has neither peace nor privacy in the house. She is disgusted with the busy, mechanical life devoid of love. She feels that even her children are alien to her and that she cannot relate to them in any way. Tired of all these relationships, she reflects:

> She would lie still, still—she would be a charred tree trunk in the forest, a broken pillar of marble in the desert, a lizard on a stone wall. A tree trunk could not harbour irritation, nor a pillar annoyance. She should imitate death, like a lizard. No one would dare rouse her. (23)

Desai uses apt imagery to bring home Nanda's yearning for isolation and tranquility. A shattered marble pillar or a lizard on a wall symbolises her sense of seclusion. Bidding farewell to her breathlessly hectic life, she seeks seclusion and loneliness. In other words, she alienates herself from the society to preserve her "self." She gives up her obscure existence and finally decides to settle at Carignano, her hillside home in Kasauli after the death of her husband. "The death of her husband is the death of her jailer. It brings her the long-laboured freedom from the condemned cell for spiritual annihilation."[35] This hillside summer villa is situated in the foothills of the Himalayas. Manori of *Where Shall We Go This Summer?* becomes Carignano in this novel from which the heroine never retreats. She is rather forced to stay there to preserve and express wholeness and sanity in the times of a heart-rending desolation caused by human world. Nanda Kaul's love of loneliness results from her disgust with the past and her awareness of a decaying life. Her husband's unfaithfulness and her children's betrayal create a spiritual vacuum in her life. So, she shifts to Carignano, her asylum-cum-home. Carignano becomes her land of freedom and joy. This place also stands for a life without illusions, colour, emotion and anxiety. Its barrenness and starkness suggests freedom from all that is indifferent to human situation. Narendra Kumar says: "It [*Fire on the Mountain*] conveys . . . an image of emptiness and sterility, an image of Nanda Kaul's loneliness and her inability to make contact. The novel is a striking image of the difficulty of communication between Nanda Kaul, the protagonist, and the milieu in which she exists."[36]

Nanda Kaul shuts herself at Carignano. She likes its loneliness and starkness. She feels happy here at the emptiness of the house. She wants to be left alone with the pines and cicadas. She wants to be left untouched and undisturbed:

> Everything she wanted was here, at Carignano, in Kasauli. Here, on the ridge of the mountain, in this quiet house. It was the place, and the time of life, that she had wanted and prepared for all her life—as she realized on her first day at Carignano, with a great, cool flowering of relief—and at last she had it. She wanted no one and nothing else. Whatever else came, or happened here, would be an unwelcome intrusion and distraction. (3)

Nanda also wants self-isolation as she despises almost everyone who comes her way: her haughty and complacent daughter, Asha, her weak and unhappy grand-daughter Tara, her elusive and sickly great grand-daughter Raka, her old and emaciated companion Ila Das. She hates any intrusion including that of a letter which the postman brings. Even memories seem to violate her solitude:

> Looking down, over all those years she had survived and borne, she saw them, not bare and shining as the plains below, but like the gorge, cluttered, choked and blackened with the heads of children and grandchildren, servants and guests, all restlessly surging, clamouring about her. (17)

The word "survived" conveys what ordeal it must have been for her to put up with the domestic routine. Such overwhelming business never gave her opportunity to express her "self."

Nanda Kaul's solitude and privacy are disturbed by the arrival of her great granddaughter, Raka. She looks upon Raka as an intruder, an unwelcome guest in her alienated world. Interestingly, Raka too shares Nanda's sense of seclusion. Both try to safeguard their spirit of independence and their sense of seclusion. The old woman and the child live together under the same roof, each guarding her independence and privacy from the other. Both of them are identified as components of the barrenness and stillness of the Carignano garden.

While Nanda's seclusion is deliberate and self-imposed, there is an air of spontaneity about Raka's privacy. Raka avoids communicating with her great grandmother and spends most of her time roaming about the ridges, dark groves and varines, watching thorny bushes, plants and trees. Like Nanda, Raka wants only one thing: "to be left alone and pursue her own secret life amongst the rocks and pines of Kasauli" (48). While Nanda's love of privacy has originated from her being sick of leading a long life of duty and obligation, Raka's is natural and instinctive. "If Nanda Kaul was a recluse out of vengeance for a long life of duty and obligation, her great grand-daughter was a recluse by nature, by instinct" (48).

A queer situation develops as Nanda and Raka have to live under the same roof physically and spiritually as well and at the same time keep themselves aloof from each other. But this does not last long. The facade of Nanda's alienation and seclusion gives way to a positive change after the arrival of Raka. In spite of her best efforts, she is irresistibly drawn to her great grand-daughter. She finds more than an equal in Raka who becomes her alter-ego. Unlike other children, "Raka has a peculiar trait of independence which fascinates Nanda. What the older lady has striven to do artfully, the child seems to do effortlessly."[37] She is not a normal child. Her interest in the wildness of nature and her wandering in the bushes, trees on the Kasauli hills even in the dark without any fear distinguish her from the other children of her age. She finds darkness "much friendlier." She is in a constant search for new experiences. She visits the village in the valley and watches the women threshing corn, treading cattle calmly. She does not like human company: "Mostly she saw no one. She had the gift of avoiding what she regarded as dispensable" (63). Raka exults in being alone. "I'm shipwrecked and alone. She clung to a rock in my boat, alone in my boat on the sea, she sang" (61-62).

Raka has passed through the nightmare of depressing childhood. She has observed her father's bad habits and his regular visits to the clubs and entertainments, and his ill-treatment of her mother. In Kasauli, running away from the club to escape the loathsome sight of revelries, she sobs reminded of her father's visits to clubs. Raka says:

> Somewhere behind them, behind it all, was her father, home from a party, stumbling and crashing through the curtains of night, his mouth opening to let out a flood of rotten stench, beating at her mother with hammers and fists of abuse—harsh, filthy abuse that made Raka cower under her bedclothes and wet the mattress in fright. (71)

So Raka develops hatred towards the world that has spoiled her father. The revelries and the other evils associated with social life in clubs play a significant role in making Raka unsocial. The marital disharmony of her parents is the major cause for her living at Carignano. Before sending Raka to Carignano, Nanda's daughter Asha writes her a letter stating that the reasons for sending the child to her is the marital disharmony between Tara and her husband Rakesh, a diplomat but a brute. Both Nanda and Raka who are deprived of security in society and fulfilment of love, live in seclusion.

Nanda begins to feel that the only person fit to inherit Carignano is Raka. In her desire to meet Raka on her own terms and also to develop a rapport with the child, Nanda proposes to visit Monkey point. They walk awkwardly together, stiffly through the entire journey. They enjoy the trip and come back to the house. At this juncture enters Ila Das, Nanda's schoolmate and a childhood friend. She is a devoted social welfare officer in a village. The arrival of Ila Das intensifies Nanda's depression. She thinks that "it would be better to have the telephone removed than risk another shock" for Ila Das keeps phoning frequently in her shrill voice. To avoid Das's disgusting voice which is no better than a cackle, Nanda invites her over for tea the following day. The event of Ila's coming for tea to meet Raka is the lull before the storm. It brings the three characters into contact before the actual climax.

Ila talks about her life. She tells them that her two brothers who are drunkards are responsible for the collapse of the family. When their father passed away, the sons did not even attend the funeral since nothing was left for them to inherit. Ila works as a teacher but later resigns the job out of her disgust with the administration. Subsequently, she becomes the welfare officer on a meagre income in a remote village. The miserable condition of Ila evokes Nanda's sympathy for her. She wants to say "come and stay with me, Ila, and then clutched it tighter still to keep herself from saying what would ruin her existence here at Carignano. She simply shook her head" (127). Then, the tea party is over. Ila Das returns home unaware of the impending danger. On the way in the night she is waylaid, raped and murdered by Preet Singh, a villager when she stops the marriage of his younger sister to an old widower. The police officer, Mr. P.K. Shukla, of Garkhal Thane informs Nanda Kaul about Ila's death over the telephone and requests her to come and identify Ila's dead body. Nanda Kaul is terribly shocked and dazed when she receives the news of the rape and the brutal murder of Ila Das. The knowledge of Ila's death gives an impetus to Nanda's own psychological destruction. Ila's death is too stark a reality for Nanda to face and so it results in her own death. "It choked and swelled in her throat. She twisted her head, then hung it down, down, let it hang" (145). Raka's unconscious desire for violence makes her set the forest on fire. Then she returns to Carignano and finds Nanda Kaul dead:

> Look, Nani, I have set the forest on fire. Look, Nani—look—the forest is on fire. Tapping, then drumming, she raised her voice, then raised her head to look in and saw Nanda Kaul on the stool with her head hanging, the black telephone hanging, the long wire dangling. (145)

Raka realises that the shock Nanda received was greater than any she received in her life. Nanda faints; the psychological defence is shattered. She does not recover from her swoon. Metaphysically, the death of Ila and Nanda are interpreted as the final reality suggesting the futility of human existence. Ila dies because of her concern for others, Nanda dies because of her concern for her loneliness. Both self-adjustment and self-alienation signify a tragic sense of unfulfilment. Feminist criticism spots out a social reality in their deaths, signifying the social forces which destroy women from within.

The mountain fire set by Raka is symbolic of the destruction of Nanda's world of fantasy. Raka's advent at Carignano set-up intensifies the subterranean conflict in Nanda Kaul. So Raka completes the process she has initiated by setting the forest on fire. The secret forest of Nanda's dreams and desires and the wilful thinking lying in the dark recesses of her psyche are destroyed by the fire of blazing truth. There is no hope for Nanda Kaul either in the external world or in the inner world which are completely destroyed. Like Maya in *Cry, the Peacock*, Nanda Kaul is estranged from both the worlds. The difference between the two protagonists is that while Maya is in a stage of mindless oblivion, Nanda Kaul is aware of her destruction.

There is a deep sense of marital dissonance in the novel. The question of male-domination also plays a vital role in disturbing the marital life. In the novel, Nanda's death as well as Ila's rape-murder points to the process of disintegration of social, economic, psychological, emotional, ethical and spiritual values of a woman who suffers in this male-dominated society. Desai explodes female freedom as a myth in most of her novels. The heroines in the novels, after an unsuccessful futile attempt at fulfilment through their quest for personhood, either die like Monisha in *Voices in the City*, or compromise their search like Sita in *Where Shall We Go This Summer?* or even stake their sanity like Maya in *Cry, the Peacock*. It seems woman has no escape in this male-dominated patriarchal family system which sanctions security to woman who submit to escape from freedom and prefer living like slaves losing their identity as individuals.

The novel *Fire on the Mountain* incorporates a bizarre psychology. In her frustration, Nanda frantically searches for self-alienation. Life has not honoured her claims. As her original self-effacing solution has not worked throughout, she substitutes it with the strategy of self-adjustment to self-alienation. Nanda, in her married life, submits herself mutely to the demands and commands of her husband but after the death of her husband she prefers self-alienation.

The conclusion is therefore, utterly despairing in this novel. Life in Desai's world is full of anguish and suffering which cannot be avoided. At the same time one has to realize the inevitability of death. Therefore, the struggle in between seems to be absurd, futile and meaningless. Nanda Kaul wishes to quit the world but the world does not leave her; she wants to forget her past life, but she cannot. Her past life ever haunts her. She is quite reluctant to allow Raka to live with her, but once she starts living with her she does not want her to leave. She does not want Ila Das to intrude into her privacy but she fails to resist. Such dichotomy in the lives and attitudes of the female protagonists of Desai's novels brings home the profound message that life becomes a torture if one does not learn to reconcile one's self to its realities. For a person of no compromise, the end of the pursuit is either insanity or death. Nanda dies under the weight of her quilt. Her death is however a redemptive death. She dies fully aware of her quilt. It is her mistake because she moves from a long period of self-adjustment to self-alienation. The marital dissonance of Nanda is not the result of emotional breakdown but that of planned and programmed breakdown. Therefore, Nanda does not commit suicide like Maya or Monisha. Her death-wish works on her psyche and it finally causes her psychic death, followed by a sudden physical demise.

### 4. From Escapism to Realism: *In Custody*

Anita Desai's forte is the portrayal of feminine characters. She tries to study in-depth their psyche. *In Custody*[38] is in a different category in the sense that she attempts to study the helpless nature of the male protagonist due to poverty, helplessness and lack of initiative. This novel also marks a departure from the earlier novels of Anita Desai. *Clear Light of Day* (1980), its immediate predecessor, has a female protagonist belonging to an upper middle class family settled in Delhi. The novel explores the sensibility of the protagonist within the framework of her disintegrating household while the world outside scarcely figures in this exploration. *In Custody* has a male protagonist who comes from a lower middle class family and whose consciousness is essentially directed towards a wider world beyond himself and his family. In doing so, Desai evokes the dominant attributes of contemporary Indian society through the character of Deven who acquires symbolic connotations besides his role as the central figure. The diverse trends that affect the contemporary middle class Indian are unified into the sensibility of the protagonist, Deven. Deven is a lecturer in Hindi in Lala Ram Lal College, Mirpore. He seeks to reach out into the wider world in the hope of self-fulfillment. He undergoes experiences of various shades and complexities and eventually emerges as a wiser man with a more complete knowledge of being in this world. But while undergoing these experiences, he suffers from the problem of marital dissonance. Deven's wife Sarla's dreams about marriage are dashed after her marriage with a low-salaried lecturer. Academically Deven is at his lowest ebb for he could not command the attention of his students. His position in the classroom is so bad that he cannot look straight in the eyes of his students. Instead, he "had been for years practising" the trick of focusing:

> His eyes upon the door at the far end of the room, the door that opened on to the passage, freedom and release. (12)

In order to tide over the situation, he ignores his class and speaks "to himself, or some one outside, invisible." (12) According to Bipin B. Panigrahi and Viney Kirpal "Deven is portrayed as a marginal character, dangling on the periphery of action incapable of forcing his way to the centre of things."[39] Deven is described as "a boring teacher"(13). He finds his job and his family oppressive and believes that he is chained to the necessity of earning a livelihood in order to support his family. His desire for freedom from mundane existence is also visible in the romantic notions he fosters about himself and his job. Such an assumption has imparted to him a sense of defeat which prevents him from total absorption in his ill-paid profession. Deven's sense of despair on the professional front finds its ripples in his domestic life as well:

> Deven had been more a poet than a professor when he married Sarla—he had only been taken on as a temporary lecturer and still had confidence in his verse—and for the wife of a poet she seemed too prosaic. Of course she had not been his choice but that of his

> mother and aunts, crafty and cautious women: She was the daughter of a friend of an aunt's, she lived on the same street as that family, they had observed her for years and found her suitable in every way: plain, penny-pinching and congenitally pessimistic. (67)

Deven comes from Delhi and settles down at Mirpore, a small town, along with his wife Sarla and son Manu and leads an unhappy domestic life. The place she lives looks like a "cruel trap or prison, as well, an indestructible prison from which there was no escape [for him]" (19). He is disappointed with the atmosphere of the institution.

> After he graduated and married and came to Mirpore to teach, it became for him the impassable desert that lay between him and the capital with its lost treasures of friendships, entertainment, attractions and opportunities. It turned into that strip of no man's land that lies around a prison, threatening in its desolation. (24)

On the other hand as a young girl and as a bride, Sarla had the usual aspirations of her girl friends, to own the three f's: "'Fan, phone, frigidaire!' they would shout whenever anyone mentioned a wedding, a bridegroom, a betrothal, and dissolve in hectic laughter" (67). But by marrying into the academic profession and by living in a small town, all her dreams had been rudely swept away:

> The thwarting of her aspirations had cut two dark furrows from the corners of her nostrils to the corners of her mouth, as deep and permanent as surgical scars. The droop of her thin, straight hair on either side of head repeated these twin lines of disappointment. They made her look forbidding and perhaps that was why her husband looked so perpetually forbidding, even if he understood their cause. (68)

Disappointment, however, had not brought them any closer. To live on a lecturer's salary can be an oppressive experience and having no choice of their own, Deven and Sarla feel desperate. On the familial front, Deven finds himself as an angry self. The repressive atmosphere of a lower middle class ethos offers him no suitable avenues for recognition. He is a gifted young man whose imagination has been fired by the glories of Urdu poetry. The harsh realities of life produce in him intense feelings of frustration and resentment and force him to adopt different solutions to cope with his difficulties. Deven is aware of his personal incompetence to fulfil his wife's desires and dreams on the material level. Like his father, he feels apologetic because he cannot do better. He lives with a sense of defeat and failure:

> He understood because, like her, he had been defeated too; like her, he was a victim. Although each understood the secret truth about the other, it did not bring about any closeness of spirit, any comradeship, because they also sensed that two victims ought to avoid each other, not yoke together their joint disappointments. A victim does not look to help from another victim: he looks for a redeemer. At least Deven had his poetry; she had nothing, and so there was an added accusation and bitterness in her look. (68)

Sarla also becomes a victim in her married life. Her high expectations about married life are dashed after the marriage.

> She dreamt the magazine dream of marriage; herself, stepping out of a car with a plastic shopping bag full of groceries and filling them into the gleaming refrigerator, then rushing to the telephone placed on a lace doily upon a three-legged table and excitedly ringing up her friends to invite them to see a picture show with her and her husband who was beaming at her from behind a flowered curtain. (68)

Deven feels inferior owing to his diffused sense of failure. Overtly, his irritability with Sarla appears to be the outcome of his hurt male ego. Deep down, his rage is, in a way, an externalization of self-hate, born out of an unconscious self-accusation. He reproaches himself for his inadequacy to make his distinction in life "all he could measure up to was this—this shabby house, its dirty corners, its wretchedness and lovelessness" (67). What he had secretly dreamt of was "the world of drama and revolving lights and feasts and furies" (67).

A contrast to "thrifty," "domesticated" Deven is Siddiqui, his colleague, a Muslim lecturer in Urdu, a bachelor, a hedonist and a romantic who has the "talent for remaking fact into more acceptable, more attractive victim." Thus, when he discovers that he cannot make both ends meet or maintain the disintegrating old *haveli*, his ancestral home, he sells it off to a Delhi-based businessman who wants to "develop" that land, by "all kinds of plans for putting his wasteland to use."

Yet another contrast to Deven is Murad, his childhood friend, now in Delhi. To Deven, Murad, the son of a wealthy Kashmiri carpet-seller, had been the rich spoilt boy with lots of money to spend on films and cigarettes while Deven had been a poor widow's son "who could be bribed and bought to do anything for him." Yet their friendship had stood the test of time. Murad is the editor of an Urdu journal, *Awaaz*, which he says he runs to save the glorious traditions of Urdu from being extinguished by the Hindi-wallas. He is probably not very rich now—he says that his father has disinherited him. Unlike Deven, he is resourceful and aggressive and seems to give the impression that he can have his way with most people. Even so, there is something quite pitiable about his attempts to get things out of people and maintain an appearance of decent living.

The motif of despair, failure, and mediocrity that underlines the lives of each of these people is repeated in several situations in the novel—in the kind of homes, D/II type, that Deven and other low-paid employees in the same grade live in; in the alienating colonial system of education mirrored in the set-up of Lala Ram Lal College, Mirpore; in the attempts to teach the languages in a scene dominated by science studies; in the phenomenon of "braindrain" and migration to more prosperous countries for lucrative jobs and other "goodies." (185-86)

Murad frequently visits Deven's college and disturbs him for company. Deven finds himself in a tight corner when he has to oblige his friend's request on one hand and guard his image as a teacher on the other. It is evident that Deven cannot discard his friendship with Murad because of his attachment to him. At the same time, he feels guilty when his students find him in the company of Murad at the college canteen and restaurant and everywhere.

Deven leads the life of a victim, a victim of the ordinary life. Whenever he sees Sarla, he is reminded of a victim figure. Tired of pursuing such a life of victimization, Deven lies low and remains invisible. He exists in an invisible cell on the margin of life. For him the countryside between Mirpore and Delhi "turned into no man's land that lies around a prison, threatening in its desolation" (24). Real life is lost to Deven.

The real and free life has always been beyond Deven's reach. The lack of togetherness combined with his idea of being a victim alienates him both from his wife and his only child, Manu. In a desperate attempt to escape from a terrible sense of isolation and marital dissonance, he seeks refuge in the fantasy-world of Urdu poetry. At this critical juncture Murad asks Deven to go to Delhi and interview Nur Shahjehanbadi, the greatest living Urdu poet of Delhi—though no longer very active—and to write an article for a special number he proposes to bring out on the poet. For Deven, lover of Urdu poetry and admirer of Nur, this becomes the very summons he has been waiting for all these years. In the first interview Deven faces humiliation at Nur's hands. Nur shouts at Deven for disturbing his sleep and calls Deven a fool: "It can only be a great fool. Fool, are you a fool?" Deven admits humiliatingly that he is a fool: "Sir, I am! I am!" (38). Again, when Nur gathers from Deven that Deven has a highly-developed taste for Urdu, Nur comes down heavily on Deven: "You don't look fit to serve anyone, let alone the muse of Urdu" (43). Nur continues his tirade against Deven: "It seems you have been sent here to torment me, to show me to what depths Urdu has fallen. All right then, show me, let me know the worst!" (43)

Deven is ready to bear the brunt of Nur's misconception and conceitedness expecting the real and free world of Nur's poetry.

This hope is shattered by cruel fate. Nur's admirers rush in and disturb the proceedings. After sharing the Jama Masjid food, spiced *Kebabs, Korma, Kofta* and drink with his admirers, Nur starts decrying Hindi and the latest poem by Sri Gobind on cycle. At the end there is another instance of humiliation for Deven. Imtiaz Begum, Nur's second wife, lashes out at Deven pointing out at the drunken Nur who collapses on the ground:

> You have reduced him to that, making him eat and drink like some animal, like a pig, laughing at your jokes, singing your crude songs, when he should be at work, or resting to prepare himself for work. (60)

Chance which thwarts Deven's efforts in the form of Imtiaz Begum is one of the invisible forces that play havoc with one's life. Kermode refers to John Cage [US Composer] to say that purposelessness is the final effect desired in a work of art.[40] It is a chance that renders anything purposeless. Purposelessness or chance may be taken as one of the characteristics of modern existence as it foils man's attempts to make his life real and certain. Thomas Hardy showed the world the dark side of chance in human existence. Similarly Anita Desai reveals, in *In Custody*, the workings of chance in Deven's life on a lower key. During the next poetic recital by Nur, Deven arranges a tape recorder and secures the services of Chiku for recording. But chance intervenes and prevents Nur's poetry from being recorded. When Nur recites poetry, Chiku would be fumbling with the machine. On the other hand at a time when Nur is flippant on unpoetic subjects, Chiku records it. At times Chiku falls asleep out of exertion, then Nur bursts out in poetry thus making the recording programme useless.

Deven ultimately becomes an embodiment of failure and frustration in pursuing his project. Murad is partly responsible for this. A.N. Dwivedi rightly remarks that "Murad is a very cunning and crafty fellow."[41] By listening to the advice given by Murad, Deven is at a loss to find a truly sympathetic soul to console him. Murad's wicked plans make Deven totally nervous and he loses interest in his literary work. He leads a life of defeat and failure and his aspirations remain unfulfilled.

While Maya in *Cry, the Peacock*, Monisha in *Voices in the City*, Sita in *Where Shall We Go This Summer?* and Nanda Kaul in *Fire on the Mountain* suffer on account of marital dissonance in a man-dominated world, Sarla of *In Custody* finds satisfaction under the care and guidance of her husband, Deven. But Deven is himself a helpless person. He understands the problems of his wife, but he cannot sort them out due to his own inadequacies in terms of tact and worldly wisdom. Sarla is a victim of her husband's weaknesses and helplessness.

J.P. Tripathi feels that "Sarla is the typical Hindu wife, simple, timid, obscure, domineered, undemanding and cooperative."[42] Their marital life is disturbed and marred by indifference and impassivity due to Deven's stupidity. The first and foremost reason for Deven's failure is his poverty. He fails to provide basic requirements to the family and things needed by his wife and son. Secondly, as he is brought up in an orthodox environment, he wants to adhere to principles and morals. His love of Urdu poetry and his obsession with name and fame make him neglect his wife. Commenting on this aspect of the problem, Anita Desai observes:

> At least Deven had his poetry, she had nothing, and so there was an added accusation and bitterness in her look. (68)

The hearts of Deven and Sarla are filled with agony and unfulfilled desires but nobility lies in them as they never complain seriously or grumble despite many hurdles. There is marital dissonance between them and also a sense of feeling for coexistence to avoid the breakage of sacred marital ties. Their thinking and their background kept them on the track of married life. Sarla observes that Deven feels like a trapped animal. He is economically hard pressed and is unable to fulfil the demands of his wife and child. His initial failure in the interview brings sorrow.

One night during summer all three of them sleep in a room enduring suffocation. Sarla is not interested in shifting cots to the courtyard as she had a nightmare of robbers attacking them in sleep. The following conversation between the couple reveals how wretched a life they are forced to live:

> What can robbers find in our house to steal? She hissed. 'To them college teachers are big men, important men; how can they know that we starve?' . . . He recalled the time he had refused to buy the child toffees when they were out shopping and she had said, through pinched lips, 'For your own son you have no money, only for going to Delhi to enjoy yourself there is money.' (130)

Sarla is convinced that Deven does not treat her properly. These circumstances make Deven neglect his family. The result is: Sarla experiences terrible dissatisfaction in her married life. As a husband, Deven has provided basic things but not the desired things for Sarla. She wants to lead a harmonious life. But poor Deven is busy with recordings and frequent visits to Delhi to meet Nur for the publication of articles in Murad's magazine. Sarla wants Deven to be the custodian of her family. But, unfortunately, he pays little attention to his marital life.

The frequent breakdown of his plans and programmes upsets him and makes him nervous. However, he continues his ceaseless efforts to succeed in his literary ambitions. Under these circumstances, Deven helplessly slips into the hands of Murad and others letting the situation go beyond his control. Dwivedi rightly remarks that he "lives in a dream-world, behaves like an innocent angel, and in the end faces a hostile world of harsh realities around him." (117) Consequently, Deven experiences failure and frustration of bitterness and restlessness.

While Deven allows himself to be trapped in the custody of Nur's poetry, his wife Sarla opts to be in his custody without being able to realize her aspirations. Thus both remain "in custody" of hostile forces over which they have no control. Viney Kirpal rightly observes: "Desai's *In Custody* is different from her other novels. Although the pervading philosophy in the novel is not similar to R.K. Narayan's (his is more in the traditional, Hindu metaphysical strain while hers is for a life that has to be faced squarely, with courage, integrity and responsibility), the novel ends on a note of hope and optimism. It evokes through creative language, structures and technique, an image of India that belies the impression of a "dead," "stagnant" India. *In Custody* offers an image of India that is full of hope and that transcends that superficial irritants that many Anglo-Indian novelists have referred to—the heat and dust of India. It is a beautiful novel by a great Indian woman writer."[43]

Finally, Deven transcends his personal problems and gains in awareness of the existential problems of man. He accepts the human condition as it is and attains the existential dimension of personality.

In *Cry, the Peacock*, Maya becomes hysterical because of a frustrated married life with Gautama, kills him and kills herself. Such frustration continues in *Voices in the City* where Monisha gets disgusted with the whole negative domestic situations of her husband's behaviour and the behaviour of her in-laws, she commits suicide. Sita in *Where Shall We Go This Summer?* suffers because of Raman's rationalistic approach and pragmatism, wants to be at Manori island to absorb her fifth child in her womb, but realises the inevitability of the natural phenomenon of childbirth, finally retreats to Bombay to adjust with her husband. In *Fire on the Mountain*, Nanda Kaul adjusts throughout her life with her husband. Mr. Kaul, who is involved in a love affair with Miss David but gets unattached with the children, goes to Carignano, dies of shock at the news of the rape and murder of her childhood friend. Deven in *In Custody* initially escapes from the domestic life for financial crisis, goes to the fantasy of Urdu poetry but realises the harsh reality of married life and responsibilities, comes back to his wife and his son Manu. Thus, Desai presents marital dissonance with a difference in her novels.

## NOTES

1 Jasbir Jain, "An Interview with Anita Desai," *Stairs to the Attic: The Novels of Anita Desai* (Jaipur: Printwell, 1987), p. 14.

2 Ramesh K. Srivastava, ed., *Perspectives on Anita Desai* (Ghaziabad: Vimal, 1984), p. xxiii.

3 Seema Jena, *Voices and Vision: Anita Desai* (New Delhi: Ashish, 1989), p. 34.

4 Anita Desai, *Cry, the Peacock* (Delhi: Orient Paperbacks, 1993).

5 Meena Belliappa, *Anita Desai: A Study of Her Fiction* (Calcutta: Writers' Workshop, 1971), p. 25.

6 Darshan Singh Maini, "The Achievement of Anita Desai," *Indo-English Literature*, ed. K.K. Sharma (Ghaziabad: Vimal, 1977), p. 216.

7 R.S. Sharma, *Anita Desai* (New Delhi: Arnold-Heinemann, 1981), p. 24.

8 K.K. Sharma, "In Search of Anti-hero: Anita Desai and Arun Joshi," *Indian English Literature: A Perspective* (Ghaziabad: Vimal, 1976), p. 174.

9 Sigmund Freud (1856-1939), born at Freiberg in Moravia, of a Jewish family, is known as the inventor of psychoanalysis. He studied under the great neurologist Charcot in Paris, and undertook with Dr. Breuer the investigation of hysteria from a psychological standpoint. The study of neurotic ailments led him to various conclusions relating to the normal mind, which are the basis of psycho-analysis, such as the existence of an unconscious element in the mind which influences consciousness, and of conflicts in it between various sets of forces (including represssion), also the importance of a child's semi-consciousness of sex as a factor in mental development.

10 Sigmund Freud, *Civilized Sexual Morality and Modern Nervous Illness*, trans. James Strachey (Harmondsworth: Penguin, 1985), p. 47.

11 Sudhakar Ratnakar Jamkhandi, "The Artistic Effects of the Shifts in points of view in Anita Desai's *Cry, the Peacock*," *The Journal of Indian Writing in English*, IX, No. 1 (Jan. 1981), p. 37.

12 Ramesh K Srivastava, ed. "Anita Desai at Work: An Interview," *Perspectives on Anita Desai*, p. 218.

13 Shanta Acharya, "Problems of the Self in the Novels of Anita Desai," *Explorations in Modern Indo-English Fiction*, ed. R.K. Dhawan (Delhi: Bahri, 1982), p. 241.

14 B. Ramchander Rao, *The Novels of Mrs. Anita Desai: A Study* (New Delhi: Kalyani, 1972), p. 9.

15 *The Geeta* philosophy was an important frame of extra literary reference in Anita Desai's earlier novels. When asked by Jasbir Jain whether it reflected her strong sense of religion, she replies: "It [the religious attitude] belonged to a certain time of my life, and it is there in my earlier books [of which *Cry, the Peacock* is the first]" Jasbir Jain, in interview with Anita Desai, p. 13.

16 Anita Desai, *Voices in the City* (Delhi: Orient Paperbacks, 1968).

17 A.V. Krishna Rao, "*Voices in the City*: A Study," *Perspectives on Anita Desai*, ed. Ramesh K Srivastava, p. 162.

18 H.M. Williams, *Indo-Anglian Literature: A Survey* 1800-1970 (Madras: Orient Longman, 1976), p. 88.

19 Ramesh K Srivastava, *Perspectives on Anita Desai*, p. 169.

20 Usha Bande, *The Novels of Anita Desai* (New Delhi: Prestige, 1988), p. 68.

21 Anita Desai, *Where Shall We Go This Summer?* (New Delhi: Orient Paperbacks, 1982).

22 Atma Ram, "Anita Desai," *Interviews Indian-English Writers*" (Calcutta: Writers' Workshop, 1983), p. 27.

23 T.S. Anand, "*Where Shall We Go This Summer?* Anita Desai's Stance against Negativism," *Language Forum*, Special Issue on Anita Desai, vol. 14, No. 1, Jan.-June 1988, p. 100.

24 Atma Ram, "An Interview with Anita Desai," *World Literature Written in English*, XVII (April 1977), p. 97.

25 S.P. Swain and P.M. Nayak, "*Where Shall We Go This Summer?*: Sita's Incarcerated Self," *The Journal of Indian Writing in English*, vol. 22, No. 1, January, 1994, p. 22.

26 Vimala Rao, "Anita Desai's *Where Shall We Go This Summer?*: An Analysis," *Commonwealth Quarterly*, vol. 3, No. 9 (1978), p. 47.

27 J.G. Masilamani, "Feminism in Anita Desai," *Kakatiya Journal of English Studies*, Vol. III, No. 1, 1978, p. 29.

28 Usha Bande, p. 116.

29 Kunj Bala Goel, *Language and Theme in Anita Desai's Fiction* (Jaipur: Classic, 1989), p. 27.

30 Atma Ram, "An Interview with Anita Desai," p. 98.

31 Anita Desai, *Fire on the Mountain* (New Delhi: Allied, 1977).

32 Shyam M. Asnani, "The Theme of Withdrawal and Loneliness in Anita Desai's Fire *on the Mountain," The Journal of Indian Writing in English*, vol. 9, No. 1 (1981), p. 82.

33 Shanta Acharya, p. 245.

34 Jasbir Jain, "An Interview with Anita Desai," *Rajasthan University Studies in English*, XII (1979), p. 12.

35 P.F. Patil, "The Theme of Marital Disharmony in the Novels of Anita Desai," *Indian Women Novelists*, ed. R.K. Dhawan, (New Delhi: Prestige, 1991), set I, vol. II, p. 139.

36 Narendra Kumar, "Novel as Image: *Fire on the Mountain* as a Tragic Farce," *The Literary Criterion*, vol. XXIX, No. 2 (1994), pp. 25-26.

37 Chandra Ganguli, "*Fire on the Mountain*: An Analysis," *Commonwealth Literature*, vol. 6, No. 21 (Dec. 1981), p. 41.

38 Anita Desai, *In Custody* (London: Heinemann, 1984).

39 Bipin B. Panigrahi and Viney Kirpal, "The Dangling Man: Deven in Anita Desai's *In Custody," The New Indian Novel in English: A Study of the 1980s*, ed. Viney Kirpal (New Delhi: Allied, 1990), p. 271.

40 Frank Kermode, "Objects Jokes and Art," *20th Century Literary Criticism*, ed. David Lodge (London: Longman, 1981), p. 667.

41 A.N. Dwivedi, "A Study of Anita Desai's *In Custody: Indian Fiction in English*, ed. R.S. Pathak (New Delhi: Northern Book Centre, 1970), p. 114.

42 J.P. Tripathi, *The Mind and Art of Anita Desai* (Bareilly: Prakash, 1986), p. 144.

43 Viney Kirpal, "The perfect bubble: A Study of Anita Desai's *In Custody*," *Image of India in the Indian Novel in English*, ed. Sudhakar Pandey and Raj Rao (Bombay: Orient Longman, 1993), pp. 133-34.

Chapter IV

# Ruth Prawer Jhabvala and Anita Desai: A Comparative Study

Today there is a considerable body of fiction written by Indian English writers. In the last three decades, two Indian women novelists, Ruth Prawer Jhabvala and Anita Desai, have won world-wide recognition. There are other women novelists like Kamala Markandaya, Nayantara Sahgal, Attia Hussain, Shashi Deshpande, Shobha De and Bharati Mukherjee who have made great strides but the kind of critical attention that has been given to Ruth Prawer Jhabvala and Anita Desai is unparalleled. A comparative study of the novels of Jhabvala and Desai points out the divergences in their treatment of the theme of marital dissonance. Jhabvala treats the theme with the keener awareness of the domestic, social, cultural, economic and philosophical implications. But Anita Desai probes the influence of these factors on the psyche of the protagonists. While portraying the theme of marital dissonance, she reveals her yearning for liberation of women from patriarchal oppression.

## 1 *The Householder* and *In Custody*

In Jhabvala's *The Householder* and in Desai's *In Custody*, there is a marked similarity with regard to the central theme of marital dissonance caused by socio-economic problems in general and temperamental differences in particular. The protagonists in these two novels in terms of their profession, financial and social crises and marital dissatisfaction are identical. Prem in *The Householder* and Deven in *In Custody* run away from the domestic turmoil but return to their houses realising their responsibilities. Prem's wife Indu in *The Householder* and Deven's wife Sarla in *In Custody* express their dissatisfaction in married life but the novels ultimately end up in domestic harmony.

In Jhabvala's *The Householder*, Prem is a Lecturer who gets a very low salary and faces financial crisis in terms of adjusting money for the payment of house rent, and heeding to the demands of his wife Indu who is pregnant. In the classroom Prem is an unsuccessful teacher. Both the students and the management are unhappy with his academic performance. Thus he fails both at financial and professional fronts. The arrival of Prem's mother complicates the situation further. The mother-in-law and daughter-in-law are at loggerheads. As a householder, Prem fails to fulfil the demands of his wife. Indu is a modernist while Prem is a traditionalist. Indu treats Prem as a failure, often goes to her parents in his absence and cares the least for his formal approval. Subsequently, he seeks spiritual help in order to run away from all these complications, but the Swamy turns down his request stating that he must be a successful person first at the domestic front. This opens his mind to seek some solution to avoid such serious marital dissonance. Luckily, Indu comes back home. He cleverly manages to send his mother to his sister in Bangalore. His mother's departure adds new enthusiasm to his spirit and Indu also feels that she is the queen of the house. Thus Indu gains her freedom and equality and Prem also tries hard to make their married life a success with the faith that their first duty is to love and to be loved by each other. Now, in spite of his failure as a Lecturer, and his failure to lower the rent, he has at last proved himself as a successful "householder." Thus the novel ends with domestic harmony.

In Desai's *In Custody*, the problem between Deven and Sarla is the lack of togetherness, his low salary as a lecturer, his frustration at the domestic front, his attempt to escape from a terrible sense of isolation and his plan to seek refuge in the fantasy world of Urdu poetry where he hopes to fulfil himself. He is a noble self in society but a victim at home because Sarla as a dreamer develops many aspirations which Deven fails to fulfil. He grows schizophrenic. The harsh reality of existence produces in him a tense sensation of hostility, but he does not revolt. He realises his commitment to Nur's poetry by becoming its custodian and at the same time he realises the need for materialistic values to be extended towards his wife and son. Thus, they begin their matrimonial life with dissonance but the reconciliation in terms of earthly needs makes Deven realise the need to coexist with the family.

Deven is a mentally disturbed person like Prem and incidentally the causes are also the same. Depression is a serious mental ailment which has been depicted with great skill by both the novelists. The stages of disenchantment and marital dissonance with their situations in life, frustration, socio-economic and domestic problems ending in reconciliation and coexistence are common in both the novels.

Like Prem, Deven, the protagonist in *In Custody*, is also a Lecturer in Hindi in a private college called Lala Ram Lal College, Mirpore, near Delhi. He lives in Mirpore with his wife Sarla and son Manu. Indu in *The Householder* is pregnant but Sarla is already the mother of a child. Prem is worried about the domestic expenditure after the child is born and Deven is already in a tight financial position. Both Indu and Sarla dream of many things but their dreams are rudely swept away by the fact of their life with academics living in small houses. Both Prem and Deven are considered to be failures by their students as well as the management. Both of them are romantics and escapists. They are incapable of facing crises. Unable to change the circumstances, they seek relief in different ways. Sohan Lal helps Prem to go to the Swamy, and Murad, the editor of *Awaaz* magazine, encourages Deven to meet Nur. Prem wants to take up spiritual life and Deven wants to seek relief in his love of Urdu poetry. The Swamy does not admit Prem into spiritual line just as Deven fails to derive pleasure from Nur's poetry due to the force of circumstances.

Both Indu and Sarla go through mental trauma which allows them no peace. The scene of Indu's leaving Prem's house without the permission or knowledge of her husband in *The Householder* is a typical example of women of aggressive and emotional temperaments who suffer from marital dissonance. She comes back of her own accord as she needs the support of her husband as the would-be mother of a child. In contrast to this situation, Deven's wife, Sarla, is quite normal, submissive, plain, penny-pinching and congenitally pessimistic. She desires that her husband should take care of them with continued responsibility.

Indu is a victim partly due to the undue intervention of her mother-in-law while there is no such problem for Sarla. Prem cleverly resolves this problem by sending his mother to his sister in Bangalore while Deven reconciles with his family life with the realisation that art is not separate from life. Deven's transformation is symbolically suggested by the image of the thorn. While rushing homewards, Deven stops only to "pull a branch of thorns from under his foot" (204). He faces the thorny path to self-realisation.

The theme of marital dissonance in *The Householder* and *In Custody* has socio-economic implications and seriously affects the psyche of the characters. Both Prem and Deven face these conflicts but they realise their responsibility towards their families and the value of permanent coexistence. Thus, Jhabvala and Desai have explored the problem of marital disintegration quite efficiently. They indirectly suggest the need for marital harmony in the disturbed social setup and family life.

### 2 *Get Ready for Battle* and *Fire on the Mountain*

Jhabvala's *Get Ready for Battle* is a novel that deals with the conflict between materialism and idealism whereas hedonism and nihilism engender it in *Fire on the Mountain*. Sarla Devi, an idealist with a reformative bent of mind, in *Get Ready for Battle* is against her husband Gulzari Lal's materialistic style of functioning. In *Fire on the Mountain*, the protagonist Mrs. Nanda Kaul yields to her husband's hedonistic attitude, leads a loveless life and gets disgusted with family life. Sarla Devi gets alienated from her married life for the "otherworldliness," while Mrs. Nanda Kaul escapes the clutches of marital relationship to a place in isolation.

In *Get Ready for Battle*, the heroine Sarla Devi is a dedicated idealist devoted to the ideals of the *Gita.* It is her vocation to serve the poor and the needy. She has ceased to live with her rich husband, Gulzari Lal, because he does not share her ideals. He is an unscrupulous materialist. Disapproving of his life, she refuses him a divorce. She is a complex character. She wants her son, Vishnu, to give up his life as a business executive in her husband's company and join her in the movement helping the poor and toiling masses. But Vishnu is attracted by his father's money rather than by his mother's idealism. His wife, Mala, shrewdly coaxes him at the instance of Gulzari Lal's mistress, Kusum, to join the scheme of making fountain pens. Sarla Devi is equally unsuccessful in a wider context. She champions the rights of refugee squatters in a malodorous slum, *Bundi Busti*, in Delhi. They are in danger of being evicted to make room for a big industrial development backed by her husband in the name of progress and hygiene. Following the teachings of Lord Krishna to Arjuna in the *Gita* to continue the struggle and do the duty without caring for the consequences, Sarla Devi defends the rights of the wretched squatters to remain housed where they are. Her efforts are frustrated as the leader of the squatters is bribed to sell out the cause to Gulzari Lal. Unfortunately, her dissolute but dependent brother, Brij Mohan, intrigues with Gulzari Lal's mistress in order to get a divorce from Sarla to Gulzari Lal. Toward the end of the novel, she allows the divorce but clings to her ideals by setting off for the red-light district of old Delhi intent on reclaiming from prostitution her brother's discarded mistress. The essence of the novel is the conflict between heroic virtue and selfish sensuality and materialism.

Anita Desai's *Fire on the Mountain* too focuses sharply on these issues. Mrs. Nanda Kaul, the protagonist, decides to stay in isolation at Carignano in Kasauli situated close to the Himalayan mountains after the death of her husband, Mr. Kaul who was an ex-Vice-Chancellor. She feels free with his death as her husband was like a jailor all through. The life-long faithlessness of her husband forces Mrs. Nanda Kaul to seclusion. She considers that her marriage was purely based on the physical lust of the man. She becomes the mother of many unloved, unwanted and unattached children. She always arranges the parties and dinners as a hard-working hostess. Externally, everything seems to be smooth but internally Nanda Kaul burns with a fire of frustration because Mr. Kaul has a liaison with a mistress, Miss David, a member of the teaching staff. Mr. Kaul invites her for badminton parties, drops her back at night and comes back home. Mrs. Nanda Kaul, submissive and subservient, tolerates this to some extent but gets gradually depressed though she keeps a frozen smile on her face. She develops a sort of destructive hatred for her husband and desires a blessed widowhood without man and children around. So she settles at Carignano but Raka, her great granddaughter, joins her later for a secluded life. Her unmarried friend Ila Das's rape and brutal murder proves an unbearable shock for Mrs. Nanda Kaul resulting in her death. Raka, the radical feminist sets the mountain on fire to save this unmolested territory from the so-called modern civilization.

Gulzari Lal and Mr. Kaul are dissimilar in their aptitudes, temperaments and approach to life. Lal's main aim is to pursue materialism. He "is a mammon worshipper and has inherited a commercial outlook."[1] In contrast, Mr. Kaul, the vice-chancellor (a vice-chancellor with a vice) is "too immersed in his affair with Miss David to notice the self-sacrificing devotion of his wife."[2] Gulzari Lal's is a joint family wherein his son Vishnu, his daughter-in-law Mala and his granddaughter Priti, live with him. Since his wife leaves the house due to unbridgeable differences in ideology, he keeps a mistress, Kusum, who in turn attends to all his domestic and personal requirements. He is non-academic unlike Mr. Kaul. Mr. Kaul is a lover of pleasures and does not bother about earning money. His house is apparently teeming with plenty in everything except love for Mrs. Kaul. Like Lal, he also keeps a mistress, Miss David, Lecturer in Mathematics. Lal is content to stay away "from his exhausting idealist wife, preferring the warm illicit body of Kusum."[3] While Miss David lives in her own house with the strong support of her lover Mr. Kaul, the widow Mrs. Kusum virtually captures Mr. Lal's castle and governs the domestic affairs. Even his son and daughter-in-law are under her influence.

Sarla Devi is not only a spiritualist but also a Gandhian idealist committed to the poor. "Her consuming thirst to work for the betterment of Indian society has wrecked her marriage."[4] For the sake of her ideals, she loses her husband, son and brother. The only gain for her is spiritual peace. In contrast to Sarla Devi's personality, Mrs. Nanda Kaul is for life within the four walls. Her thirst is to gain the love of her husband. She feels that she is empty and loveless. She is not for any external reformation. All her life, Nanda lives in pretences. She is the mistress of an educated and civilized family. She is always in the hubbub of a busy whirl. She looks like the queen of the Vice-Chancellor's house. She attends on guests. She looks after "so many children" and servants, serving her husband efficiently:

> Too many trays of tea would have to be made and carried to her husband's study, to her mother-in-law's bed-room, to the verandah that was the gathering place for all, at all times of the day. Too many meals, too many dishes on the table, too much to wash up after. (29)

Thus she is engaged in her duties disavowing her pride. Hardly ever resentful, she is at the most vexed when guests pour in allowing her no privacy. Thus, she remains a silent sufferer. She thinks of the bird as "nervous and agitated." Symbolically, "she is like the bird, disturbed, agitated, unable to fight and defend herself."[5] Her visitors call her "splendid." The image of the flying bird unevenly flashes across her mind whenever her husband leaves her alone to carry on his love affair. To relieve the tension of the situation, she considers her aloneness as "a moment of private triumph, cold and proud" (26). Such of Mrs. Nanda's compulsive drives and her inability to pattern her life is in contrast to Sarla Devi's willpower and impulsive nature that takes her to hold on to her belief regardless of the consequences. Mrs. Kaul is timid, inactive, submissive and dull, but Sarla Devi is bold, dynamic, dashing, and aggressive by nature.

In *Get Ready for Battle*, Sarla Devi's son Vishnu and daughter-in-law Mala also have marital dissonance. Vishnu rejects Mala's request for allowing her to go to Bombay, where her parents live. Their life is a life of disagreement. She does not like her husband's association with the unmarried modern girls and also with the number of hooked women. The marital disintegration in Vishnu's life is mild but in contrast to this in *Fire on the Mountain* it is not Mrs. Nanda's daughter Asha but Mrs. Nanda's granddaughter Tara who suffers from severe marital dissatisfaction. Tara and her husband Rakesh, a diplomat, are at loggerheads. Rakesh's ill-treatment, his affairs with other girls, his drinking and brutality reduce Tara to a helpless jelly. Raka's traumatic experiences deprive her of a child's joy in the company of others. So, Raka is vexed with her loveless life and goes to Carignano in Kasauli to be with Mrs. Nanda. There is a loss of roots and consequently, all her actions and gestures become "senseless, absurd and useless." Mrs. Nanda is shattered with the tragic news of rape and murder of Miss Ila Das and she dies of this shock. It is difficult to disagree with Iyengar when he says: "The supreme irony is that Nanda with all her children, grandchildren and great grandchildren and the unmarried Ila equally feels utterly lonely, which perhaps is meant to show up the futility of living married or single."[6] Thus the degree of marital dissonance in case of Raka's parents is more than what we find in Pritti's parents in *Get Ready for Battle*.

Marital disharmony in *Get Ready for Battle* results from the ignorance of the fact that ideals cannot be thrust down the throats of people. Sarla Devi accepts the disharmony and her failure in helping the poor people from being 'railroaded' by her husband. She accepts the marital wreckage for the sake of ideals. Mrs. Nanda Kaul in *Fire on the Mountain* accepts and adjusts with marital dissonance for a long life during Mr. Kaul's days but after his death she gets disgusted with life and develops the concept of nihilism. Her loveless life disturbs her and she realises that life is useless as none of the family members likes and loves her. In search of isolation she goes to Carignano in Kasauli but dies of shock as her friend Ila Das is raped and murdered. While Sarla Devi is alive and goes to the red-light area in order to realise her idealistic ambitions, Mrs. Nanda Kaul goes to Carignano, lives in isolation and dies there.

### 3 *Esmond in India* and *Voices in the City*

The problem of marital dissonance is explored by Ruth Prawer Jhabvala in *Esmond in India* and Anita Desai in *Voices in the City* through different means. Jhabvala presents it from the perspective of East-West confrontation and Desai delineates it from the perspective of non-adjustment of modern female protagonist in the traditional Indian joint family that leads to self-resignation. In *Esmond in India* Gulab, an Indian housewife, leaves her husband Esmond, an Englishman, with a sense of insecurity because he fails to protect her from the servant who tries to molest her. Desai in her novel *Voices in the City* glorifies the character of Monisha who suffers from psychic turmoil because of her marriage with a prosaic dull husband, Jiban. Failing to adjust herself with the situation, she commits suicide. While Gulab takes shelter under the guardianship of her mother, Monisha decides to lead her life without seeking shelter from anybody. Both of them, however, break their marital ties after enduring their husbands for quite some time.

In Jhabvala's *Esmond in India*, Esmond is an expatriate who hates India but makes money by teaching Hindi and 'Indian Culture' to rich Indian women and English and American tourists in Delhi. He is also a gigolo. He has married a pretty, fat Indian girl called Gulab. This marriage ultimately proves that 'East is East and West is West and the twain shall never meet.' Esmond, like any other European who "creates a little Europe at home,"[7] is unhappy with Gulab's Indian attitudes to life. "He becomes crude in conversation, and even offensive. His sarcasm, his sneer, his contempt is all lost on Gulab since, with her pretty looks, she is very languorous and placid."[8] After his return from the mercenary and philandering expeditions, Esmond stoops to abusing and beating his docile wife and her child. He even seduces a young, beautiful, educated Indian girl Shakuntala who foolishly falls in love with him. Frustrated with Esmond's cruelty, Gulab returns to her mother's house with her son. Esmond abandons both Gulab and Shakuntala for his old mistress Betty who offers to pay for their joint return to England. Esmond and Betty hate India and are glad to leave the country. The Western materialistic view of Esmond comes into conflict with the Indian philosophic resignation of Gulab. Finally their marriage breaks down.

In Desai's novel *Voices in the City*, Nirode and his two sisters Monisha and Amla rebel against the stolid conventions of middle class life and long for creativity and self-expression. Each comes to grief: Nirode ends up as a drifting bohemian, Monisha commits suicide and Amla is heart-broken when her love is rejected. The story set in Calcutta presents a strange and incongruous picture of the conjugal life of Monisha. Monisha's marriage with Jiban is a miserable failure. Her relationship with her husband is marked by 'loneliness,' 'silence' and 'indifference.' Monisha feels shattered in Jiban's house by her fat mother-in-law, placid uncles and aunts. A feeling of boredom, monotony and lack of privacy torments her. The love she desires is far beyond her reach. Even ordinary communication and understanding generally seen in most of the human beings is missing in the relationship of Monisha and Jiban. In her own house, she is accused by her mother-in-law of stealing her husband's money. Her husband does not come to her rescue at this critical juncture. By nature, Monisha was morbid and her father married her off to Jiban hoping that marriage would cure her morbidity. But things take a different turn. In the hands of a formal, apathetic and bureaucratic husband Monisha discovers her life to be "'traceless,' meaningless, uninvolved" (140). Her marital relationship with Jiban collapses as she commits suicide.

Monisha's sister Amla is fascinated by Dharma who is already married but her dream is mercilessly shattered when she comes to know that he is capable of turning away his only daughter from his house for having done something unnatural and shameful. She feels that she will be unsafe in his hands and keeps away from him though she keeps her identity in Dharma's painting.

It is interesting to note that Gulab in *Esmond in India* and Monisha in *Voices in the City* are quite different temperamentally. Gulab represents the traditional Indian spirit in food habits, dressing, son's upbringing, her dutiful loyalty to Esmond, and her lack of interest in becoming a socialite. Though she is the wife of a Westerner she refuses to move with him among his friends outside the flat. She is content to be totally confined to her house and surrender to her husband. Gulab, who was a rebel and a non-conformist before the marriage, who rejected Amrit and insisted on marrying an Englishman for his alluring personality, has become a conformist after marriage and considers her husband a demigod. She meekly endures all the brutal tortures from her husband because she has married him against the wishes of her mother and it is said to be a love-marriage. In contrast, Monisha's marriage with Jiban—who is double her age—is a marriage arranged by her father against her wishes. Though Monisha is morbid and silent by nature, she has a progressive temperament. She yearns for privacy, freedom to think, freedom to speak and freedom to take decisions. She is not so obedient and submissive as Gulab. Monisha is another version of Maya. Like Maya, she too is estranged from her husband but her estrangement is constitutional and temperamental rather than socio-psychic.

Gulab lives in a flat abounding in furniture with no place on the floor to relax. Her pastime is her little son, Ravi. In a true spirit of Indian culture, she allows some suggestions to come from her mother who lives nearby. Esmond is enraged by his mother-in-law's continual interference. Gulab silently suffers. In *Voices in the City*, Monisha lives with her mother-in-law, uncles and aunts in a small house crowded with innumerable members without any chance for privacy. There is constant interference of her mother-in-law who behaves like a dictator in domestic matters. For Monisha, it is nothing but slavery. She is made to touch the feet of a large number of aunts and uncles. Later, she is confined to the activities of cooking, washing and massaging her mother-in-law's feet. This hurts her pride. The conflict between mother-in-law and daughter-in-law in *Voices in the City* and that of mother-in-law and son-in-law in *Esmond in India* is almost identical with an Indian flavour. Jhabvala also has focused on the silent hostility between mother-in-law and daughter-in-law in *The Householder*.

While Gulab is lucky to have a male child to absorb all her attention, Monisha suffers a lot due to her childlessness. "The traditional Indian society looks down upon a childless woman, and a woman gains status only as a mother."[9] Her childlessness develops a sense of inferiority complex in Monisha contributing to her marital dissonance. Gulab is obsessed with religious practices though "there is no place for religion in the smart little flat occupied by Esmond and Gulab."[10] Monisha's attention is drawn to the lines of the *Gita* which say that a man of wisdom is satisfied in the Self by the Self alone, and he has no desires. She substitutes the real self by her actualized self-image and feels assured of her non-involvement. The concept of "the Self" as mentioned in the *Gita* is deeper than what Monisha has taken it but Gulab has not bothered to take shelter under religion to console her mind because "she is conceived in an amused detachment."[11] Thus both the female protagonists suffer from marital disintegration for different reasons.

Jhabvala's Gulab surrenders to her husband for his satisfaction treating him like a demigod, but when her personal honour is assaulted by her servant she feels that her husband has failed in his duty to protect her. So she leaves Esmond's apartment never to return. Thus the failure of Gulab's marriage suggests the point of separation between the two cultures and races. In Desai's *Voices in the City*, the culture and race are the same but the reasons for disintegration are different. Jiban fails to understand Monisha's feelings and he never tries to patch up differences. Therefore, the neurotic Monisha sets fire to herself to end the despised real self. Thus, Gulab leaves Esmond's house due to East-West confrontation, but Monisha out of frustration at not finding real life commits suicide.

### 4 *A Backward Place* and *Where Shall We Go This Summer?*

Both Jhabvala in *A Backward Place* and Desai in *Where Shall We Go This Summer?* probe the theme of marital maladjustment caused by psychological conflicts in the conjugal life of the female protagonists. Both Judy, an English girl in *A Backward Place* and Sita in *Where Shall We Go This Summer?* suffer equally at the hands of their husbands but in true spirit of Indian tradition compromise with the practical situation and adjust with their husbands. The marital relations of Judy and Sita with their husbands move from compliance to rebellion and then back to compliance again.

In *A Backward Place* Jhabvala presents the problems of three expatriate women who settle down in India after independence. They come to India of their own accord as permanent residents, but they consider modern India a backward place. India's 'backwardness' is constantly assailed by Etta, a Hungarian, who, after the failure of her marriage to an Indian student, develops a love affair with an Indian businessman. Deserted by her lover Gupta, she unsuccessfully attempts to commit suicide. Finally she surrenders to living with her friend Clarissa in a flat. Clarissa, an English girl, wears sarees, imitates Indian customs, and raves about the spirituality of the East. She falls in love with the spiritual India, the India of Sri Ramakrishna and Sri Aurobindo. But she discovers that the reality of India is different from the holy India that she had read about. Her life, which was to have been the pursuit of metaphysical wisdom, has turned out to be a struggle with the climate, predatory landlords, and the need to make both ends meet. Thus they surrender to the inevitable.

The most successful surrender to India is that of Judy, an English girl married to a vain Indian, Bal. Unlike the passionate, violent and possessive Etta and the scatter-brained Clarissa, Judy is the very embodiment of common sense and Anglo-Saxon coolness. She finds Bal's large united Hindu family a tremendous relief after her small miserable family in England with its history of depression and suicide. Her problem is not nostalgia for England but a dread moving from Delhi to Bombay and a constant psychological fear of the fecklessness of her unemployed husband. It is true that Bal does not have any work to do but he has a meaningful relationship with his wife. Judy suffers from financial crises due to her husband's unemployment. She has to work as an Assistant Secretary at "Cultural Dais." Still she considers life in India not in terms of its backwardness but 'a place of peace.' Judy's pragmatism clashes with Bal's immature optimistic attitude in solving the financial and related domestic problems. She gets disgusted and develops a close association with a like-minded idealist, Sudhir Bannerji, but her friendship is disturbed with his decision to leave Delhi to take up a teaching assignment in Calcutta. Witnessing the contented resignation of her husband's pious old aunt, she realises the need to adjust with her silly husband and follows him willingly to an uncertain future in Bombay where he wants to join the film industry under the auspices of Kishan Kumar, a reputed film-actor.

Anita Desai's Sita in *Where Shall We Go This Summer?* suffers from marital maladjustment with her husband Raman due to psychic conflicts. Raman is a businessman. His attitude to life is linked with business. He ignores Sita's iconoclastic attitude. He neglects her inherent honesty that resists any such compromise.

Sita is pregnant for the fifth time. She declares, "I don't want to have the baby" (34). It is an indication of her metaphysical desire not to commit an act of violence by giving birth to a child which is now safely contained in her womb, into a world which is full of violence and destruction. Raman interprets her declaration as her wish to have an abortion; he says, "one can't have an abortion at this stage" (34). The metaphysical and spiritual level at which Sita lives is far beyond Raman's reasoning which is confined to material common sense. Her desire to escape is mainly from a doomed and destructive human predicament which is misunderstood by Raman.

The dissatisfaction proceeds primarily from their temperaments. Raman has a pragmatic view of life, while Sita is sensitive, keen-eyed, poetic and imaginative. If Raman is an extrovert, Sita is an introvert. Raman, however, does not honour her feelings and her dream is never realised. Raman finds his mundane activities more fascinating and fulfilling. He directs his energies towards his business in order to escape from intra-psychic and inter-personal conflicts. Their contradictory drives drag them apart, making it difficult for each to comprehend the motives of the other. Sita, in order to release her self-tormenting intent, goes to Manori, an island famous for miracles for the miraculous evaporation of the child. But she finds that the magic power of the island, which belonged to her childhood fantasy, has completely disappeared. This bitter realization brings her back to the painful reality forcing her to retrace her steps towards the slavish security of her house in Bombay and give birth to her child. Sita thus accepts the general philosophy that doing away with procreation is inhuman and cowardly. She realises that life is to be faced courageously with balance of mind.

Jhabvala in her novel *A Backward Place* and Desai in her *Where Shall We Go This Summer?* have shown the problem of marital dissonance caused by intra-psychic conflicts. This marital maladjustment seems to be a legacy of unhappy parents to their daughters Judy and Sita. In striking contrast, Judy's joy in her Indian family is better than the powerful reaction to her memories of her girlhood home in England where she had lived with her parents. It was a tight little house with the doors and curtains firmly shut to keep the cold and the strangers out. Her father died of lung cancer. Left alone, her mother hanged herself to death. In a similar way, Sita also has a painful history. Her father passed away at Manori island. Her mother had run away from him. Her eldest sister, Rekha and brother Jiban also left Manori leaving Sita alone there. Thus both Judy and Sita had suffered trauma during their young age.

Both Judy and Sita are motherless children. Both of them come from lower-middle class families. Bal met Judy in London where he came as an Indian delegate to a conference of International youth. She fell in love with his handsome face, married him and settled with him in a low-middle class joint family house in Delhi. In Sita's case, she is left alone at Manori. Her father's friend Deedar and his son Raman visit the place. Like Judy's marriage, Sita's marriage was settled "out of pity, out of lust, out of a sudden will for adventure and because it was inevitable, he [Raman] married her" (99). For Raman, it is not a marriage of love, for it was out of lust and passion for female beauty he had decided to marry her and luckily the situation was in his favour. Thus we find that the situations are more or less identical in the marriages of both Judy and Sita.

There are four parts in Jhabvala's *A Backward Place* and the story is interwoven covering all the parts. Desai's *Where Shall We Go This Summer?* has three parts and each part is identified with the title. Part I is entitled "Monsoon 67," wherein Sita rebels against Raman and goes to Manori. Part II, entitled "Winter 47," depicts Sita's life with her father twenty years ago. Part III, "Monsoon 67," connects Part I and refers to Raman's visit to Manori to fetch the children. Sita also decides to accompany Raman to Bombay. Her silent surrender is attributed to her withdrawal and reconciliation realising the stark realities she will have to face in future as she is the mother of four children and another child will be added to the family.

Intra-psychic conflicts play a vital role in both the novels for different reasons. The interaction between East and West is centred around Judy and Bal in *A Backward Place*. Judy is a down-to-earth realist and her life in India seems to revolve around her husband, the two children, her middle-class surroundings in Delhi, and her income of around five hundred rupees as an Assistant Secretary. Her husband's old aunt is the source of spiritual inspiration to her. She is also safe and happy with her sister-in-law Shanti and her husband's brother Mukund. She likes the joint family structure wherein she finds solace and psychological satisfaction, security and peace of mind. But her husband is a failure and a compulsive dreamer. She is worried about his immaturity and irresponsibility. Once, Prithvi, Judy's little son, has fever and wants his father to stay with him while Bal wishes to attend on Kishan Kumar, a Bombay film actor on a visit to Delhi. Judy asks Bal to procure ice:

> 'Get the ice,' she said. Prithvi obligingly started to cry for it from the bedroom. 'It is very important for me to keep up my contacts. Without contacts you can't succeed in my line. Are you getting it or not?' (25)

She catches his sleeve and asks him to do his duty as father. He yields but she is not happy with such minor triumphs. The reasons for psychic conflicts in *Where Shall We Go This Summer?* are that Sita, the mother of four children, lives with her husband's parents and relatives in a flat in Bombay. She revolts against their subhuman placidity, calmness and sluggishness. She rebels against the 'vegetable existence' of the women of Raman's family. She disrespects them by taking to smoking and behaving with a certain degree of superiority. She considers Raman's business associates as animals. "They are nothing—nothing but appetite and sex. Only food, sex and money matters. Animals" (47). This outburst vexes Raman who is "not an introvert, nor an extrovert—a middling kind of man . . . dedicated unconsciously to the middle way." ( 47).

We find some degree of rebellious attitude both in Judy and Sita. Judy depends on Sudhir Bannerji for her job security as her boss Mrs. Kaul, who is charmed by him, would retain her till such time that he chooses to work with her at Cultural Dais. Judy also depends on Sudhir for her emotional security. Sudhir is diagonally opposite to Judy's husband, Bal. Bal is highly excitable, volatile and unabashedly optimistic. Sudhir, in comparison, is quiet and restrained. After having an excitable and voluble stay at home with her excitable husband, the quiet life in office alongside Sudhir provides Judy the right sort of balance. H.M. Williams observes, "she is tempted to enter an adulterous relationship with an idealistic like-minded Indian colleague [Sudhir] and is only saved from this sad alternative when her would-be lover abandons corrupt Delhi."[12] Similarly we find that Sita too is rebellious in her temperament: "in Sita's wish to perpetuate her pregnancy, there is a kind of rebellion right through to the last moment. She goes to Manori against all norms and advice. She becomes militantly aggressive towards all, Raman, her children and later towards Moses [servant]."[13] This single motif of not giving birth is indicative of an extremely rebellious character. In contrast it is mild and hidden in Judy.

There is a strong similarity in the way both Judy and Sita reconcile and surrender themselves to their respective predicaments under the influence of Indian spiritualism accepting the need for association and attachment with their husbands. Judy's attitude undergoes a change mainly through her contact with *Bhuaji*, a widow living with Bal. *Bhuaji*, as an obedient servant to God, takes dips in rivers, visits temples and offers prayers leaving everything to God. Like *Bhuaji*, Judy too starts saying "God provides." Judy is thrifty by nature but she hands over her savings to Bal and follows him to Bombay on his dubious adventure into the world of films. Likewise, Sita, having failed in stopping the birth of her child realises that she is caught in an existential predicament. Gradually she accepts life with her husband and children in Bombay. She also feels that the idea of escape is only a dream. It is reality she espouses at last. Just as Judy follows her husband to Bombay, Sita also follows her husband and children to Bombay.

In both the novels, thus, the return motive is much stronger than the escape. Both Indu and Sita return. Their return might simply be an index to a new beginning. Both head for Bombay—to obviously a life of promise and success but promises and successes are bound to be ambivalent and elusive. The determination, nonetheless, to continue is a clear sign of their internal capacity for endurance and reconciliation.

### 5 *Heat and Dust* and *Cry, the Peacock*

The extra-marital relationship of Olivia of Jhabvala's novel *Heat and Dust* and the emotional traumas of Maya of Desai's novel *Cry, the Peacock* cause marital disintegration in their lives. Both Jhabvala and Desai have dealt with the theme of marital dissonance though on different planes. Olivia, an English woman, is a rationalist; she gets her illegal pregnancy aborted, leaves her husband and settles down in the Himalayan mountains with the Nawab of Khatm, whereas Maya is an Indian woman. She is passionate but frustrated by the failure of her marriage, kills her husband and subsequently commits suicide. Both Olivia and Maya are victims of marital tyranny.

*Heat and Dust* is a novel about India. It tells the story of a European couple in India. Mr. Douglas Rivers is a Barrister but works as Assistant Collector at Satipur, apparently in Rajasthan. His wife Olivia suffers from alienation. Olivia of *Heat and Dust* is a complete contrast to Judy of *A Backward Place*. Olivia is a pretty, pleasure-seeking, petulant woman. She comes to India in 1923 with her husband Douglas whom she thinks she loves. But shortly after her arrival in India she meets the Nawab, feels attracted towards him and has an affair with him. Though Olivia succeeds in keeping away the heat and dust of India shutting all the doors and windows, she succumbs to the heat of passion in herself and becomes pregnant. She hides the secret from her husband and gets her pregnancy aborted for fear that the child would be easily identified as an Indian and that might prove her infidelity. Therefore, she leaves her husband and becomes the mistress of the Nawab. Douglas is shocked and finally gets a divorce. He marries Tessie. Olivia is well received by the Nawab who in turn buys a house for her in the Himalayan mountains where after six years she passes away.

The whole story is narrated in 1973 by the granddaughter of Douglas. She is the daughter of his son, born out of marriage with Tessie. The narrator comes to India to solve the enigma of Olivia's scandal. Unlike Olivia, the narrator comes to India to seek a simpler and more natural way of life but like Olivia she too develops an affair with an Indian, Inder Lal, and becomes pregnant. She prefers to have the child and settle in India. While Olivia's emotional entanglement with the Nawab was a result of her marital dissonance, the narrator's decision to live in India is a matter of choice.

Anita Desai introduces the theme of marital dissonance through her first novel, *Cry, the Peacock*, published in 1963. The degree of dissonance in this novel is so deep that the temperamental incompatibility has encroached on the lives of Maya and her husband Gautama. Maya, hypersensitive, high-strung and pampered, young wife of Gautama, loves life sensuously. She is a childless, lonely and distracted woman. She stands simply for Maya or illusion. Her private world is morbid, insane and abnormal. But when she is normal she is active and enjoys life with all its physical attractions. Gautama, a cool, practical and unsentimental advocate by profession, on the other hand, remains busy day and night, leaving his lonely wife at home with no work or friends. She longs for company. Her fertile mind weaves beautiful stories into which she temporarily withdraws. But reality is too much for her sensitivity to withstand.

The death of 'Toto,' her pet dog, disturbs Maya's sensitive mind. For Gautama it is not a serious matter. Since she is a childless woman, the memory of Toto and the resultant idea of death haunts her subconscious mind. Toto's death remains in the centre of her thinking process and that feeling takes her to the prophecy of death by an albino in her childhood. The albino astrologer predicts the death of one of the couple after four years of marriage. As a result, Maya's relations with Gautama grow worse as the years go by. Besides this the shrieking sound of the peacocks makes her restless because the cry of the peacock is synonymous with death. She knows that the peacocks dance when the sky is cloudy under the passion of life and search for mates. So, Maya feels the agony of life and death in the call of the peacocks. The cry of the peacock becomes the part of her life. But Gautama, who is guided by the *Gita* and its teachings of non-attachment, never understands her properly. Maya runs after love and Gautama flees from it. Maya suffers from both physical and mental alienation. Gautama remains aloof from her emotional and sexual urges. So, she grows hysterical.

As the days pass by, an unbridgeable gulf develops between Maya and Gautama. One day, while they walk on the roof of their house as he comes between her and the moon, she pushes him down to his death. Towards the end of the novel she explains the whole affair cryptically. "It had to be one of us, you see, and it was so clear that it was I who was meant to live. You see, to Gautama it didn't really matter. He didn't care, and I did" (215-16). She sulks with darkness all around her. Thus Maya's extreme sense of marital dissonance makes her kill her husband and commit suicide later.

Jhabvala's couple in *Heat and Dust* is the English people and Desai's couple in *Cry, the Peacock* is Indian but the sense of dissatisfaction and disaffection so pervasive in both the novels is different in its implications. Both of them feel isolated, disintegrated, dissociated and alienated with their husbands in their conjugal life. Olivia gets bored in her spacious house as Douglas, an able administrator, bears the Indian heat and dust and goes out in the morning on duty and comes late at night too tired to sit for long. Similarly, Gautama spends day and night attending to files related to his legal profession keeping Maya aloof. So the heroes of both the novels are work-conscious men. They are worried about their official duties all the time. They have a practical bent of mind whereas the heroines are creatures of emotions. In the identical situations, Olivia in London had loved having hours and hours to herself as a very introspective person and here in India she is "locked up with the servants who padded around on naked feet and respectfully waited for her to want something" (17-18), and Maya having an indulgent and somewhat over-protective childhood is unable to adjust with her husband Gautama. Her love for her father becomes an obsession. Both Olivia and Maya are childless women. This state of childlessness also adds a lot of dissonance to their married life.

With a little contrast in Olivia's life, there is no involvement of albino astrologer's prediction of death but it is there in Maya's life. Her pet dog Toto's death and peacocks' cry remind her that one of the couple would die after four years of married life. Maya suffers from this tension whereas for Olivia it is not there. In addition to this, the heroines have different tastes. They are non-conformists and want to have their own way. The heroes are conservative and like to do everything in their own ways. Olivia refuses to go to Simla though Douglas permits her to go and Maya wants to attend Kathakali dance programme but Gautama suggests that she should wait till the troupe visits their place. Thus he discourages her desire which is in contrast to Douglas' desire to send Olivia to Simla for a sojourn and to save herself from heat and dust.

Both Douglas and Olivia are keen to have children. Time passes but Olivia does not conceive. She does not ascribe her supposed infertility to any biological defect or a physical incompatibility. She comes out with a psychological reason; "she had been so frightened by all the little babies in the graveyard, dead of small pox, dead of cholera, dead of enteric fever (105). For Maya, the desire to dream for a child is beyond her imagination because Gautama simply does not understand the needs of her body and spirit. For him the real man of wisdom is "he who is free from all attachment neither rejoices in receiving the good nor is vexed on receiving evil, his wisdom is well established." Maya belongs to this world and she needs to live her full life. Gautama who indulgently quotes from the *Gita* and explains the theory of *Karma* blissfully ignores his marital responsibility towards his wife. "His [her husband's] love and sexual gratification in a normal course would have been the compensation to overcome the loss of childhood."[14]

Once the Nawab of Khatm, a state few miles away from Satipur, invites both Olivia and Douglas for dinner. Olivia is impressed very much by the palace, the dinner arrangements, the Eastern way of life, the charming Nawab, his gay and courteous manners and his romantic personality. At first sight, the Nawab rests his eyes on her and she responds positively. Later the Nawab visits Olivia's place, takes her to the shrine of Firdaus. She visits the Nawab quite frequently; these visits develop into a close friendship. She voices her dissatisfaction with Douglas who could not make her pregnant. She is eager to get pregnant. As a result of the relationship, Olivia gets pregnant, but realising her guilt she wants to go for an abortion. She also decides to leave Douglas once and for all. Olivia, after abortion, prefers to stay in the Himalayan mountain where she dies after some time. In contrast to this, Maya, true to the spirit of an Indian traditionalist, refuses to cross the orthodox ethical border of loyalty and consequently suffers. It is quite likely that their respective cultural upbringing may be responsible for the two different modes of behaviour. Olivia is a Westerner, sex taboos do not hold as strongly in her case as in the case of Maya. This accounts for Maya's intense emotional and psychological anguish, leading almost to a state of neurosis.

Olivia's socio-psychic behaviour with the delusion of the whiteman's righteous governance and the delusion of the romantic Eastern view of life create the marital dissonance and her obsession makes her a tragic victim at the Himalayas. In contrast to this, Maya gets frustrated with her discordant conjugal life, kills her husband and kills herself. However, the sense of frustration leads them to different ends.

## NOTES

1 H.S. Mahle, *Indo-Anglian Fiction: Some Perceptions* (New Delhi: Jainsons, 1985), p. 51.

2 Usha Bande, *The Novels of Anita Desai: A Study in Character and Conflict* (New Delhi: Prestige, 1988), p. 93.

3 H.M. Williams, *The Fiction of Ruth Prawer Jhabvala* (Calcutta: Writers' Workshop, 1973), p. 42.

4 *Ibid.*, p. 40.

5 Usha Bande, p. 93.

6 K.R. Srinivasa Iyengar, *Indian Writing in English* (New Delhi: Sterling, 1984), p. 745.

7 K. Meera Bai, "The Theme of East-West Encounter: The Expatriate Writer's Personal Dilemma," *Indian Women Novelists*. Set III, Vol. 3, ed. R.K. Dhawan (New Delhi: Prestige, 1995), p. 11.

8 V.A. Shahane, *Ruth Prawer Jhabvala* (New Delhi: Arnold-Heinemann, 1983), p. 87.

9 Meena Shirwadkar, *Images of Woman in Indo-Anglian Novel* (New Delhi: Sterling, 1979), p. 64.

10 Yasmine Gooneratne, *Silence, Exile and Cunning* (New Delhi: Orient Longman, 1983), p. 107.

11 Meenakshi Mukherjee, *The Twice-Born Fiction* (New Delhi: Arnold-Heinemann, 1971), p. 64.

12 H.M. Williams, "A Retrospective Look at Ruth Prawer Jhabvala's Career as a Novelist: The Indian Novels," *Passages to Ruth Prawer Jhabvala*, ed. Ralph C. Crane (New Delhi: Sterling, 1991), p. 9.

13 Usha Bande, p. 114.

14 K.C. Baral and C.K. Naik, "Desire and Death in Anita Desai's *Cry, the Peacock*," *Triveni*, vol. 61, No. 1 (Jan.-March, 1992), p. 17.

Chapter V

# Conclusion

Both Jhabvala and Anita Desai have effectively dealt with the theme of marital dissonance in all its psychological, sociological and economic ramifications. Jhabvala and Desai are pre-eminently the novelists of domestic: its joys and sorrows, its fusion and friction and its fulfilment and frustration. Bidulata Choudhury observes: "the spiritual loss paved the path for disintegration of family relations."[1] Besides this "men belonging to different professions who aspire for prosperity simply for the sake of social status and prestige are forced to face marital discords of violent type."[2] In most of the novels of Jhabvala and Desai, 'status' mars the husband and wife relationship creating a gulf between them.

Both Jhabvala and Desai have given a new direction to the fictional treatment of marital dissonance. "Jhabvala thinks that an arranged marriage does not necessarily lead to a harmonious life. There is dissonance in most of the cases."[3] Desai probes psychoanalytic factors of marital dissonance. According to K.R.S. Iyengar, Jhabvala has given us a true picture of women: "Beat them, starve them, maltreat them how you like they will sit and look with animal eyes and never raise a hand to defend themselves."[4] Both these novelists have stipulated the view that the novels are not meant to explain theories of philosophy, sociology and psychology, they are rather concerned with the disturbing questions of women existence. Women in their novels are seen as worst sufferers, highly oppressed and suppressed by social "tantalisation" or "marital dissonance." The later novels of Jhabvala and Anita Desai deal with the "trapped married couple" in which women are treated like animals and cows."[5] By sharing the same feeling and observation, Jhabvala's personality has charmed Desai to depict her characters with psychological and marital conflicts. Thus the study of human relationship is not merely of peripheral interest in the fiction of Jhabvala and Desai; rather it is central to their creative concerns. The emotional bond between man and woman is characterised in these novels of Jhabvala and Desai by dissonance and despair.

To take Ruth Prawer Jhabvala first, we find numerous impulses and tendencies in her fiction. These traits are described in Jhabvala's world. Jhabvala herself speaks about her art of characterization: "I use one character and split that character up. I have certain leading figures in my life and I seem to use them again and again, presenting different facets of their personality so one person can play role of fifty."[6] This lends authenticity to her characters. Her women characters may broadly be placed in four major categories. First, there is a woman who is both aggressive as well as submissive. Indu in *The Householder* defies her husband for the sake of her ideal of individual freedom. The Indian situation of mother-in-law versus daughter-in-law confrontation is projected in this novel. The moment Prem sends away his mother, the problem is solved and Indu becomes submissive to Prem. The second category of woman is Sarla Devi in *Get Ready for Battle* who takes a drastic step leaving her husband's house. She is aggressive as well as idealistic. We have a passive and assertive character in the third category. She is Gulab in *Esmond in India.* Gulab submits to Esmond but when the situation is beyond her control, she becomes assertive and leaves his house for her parents. In the same category, there is Judy in *A Backward Place* who is submissive but reasonable. Judy submits to Bal for all practical purposes though there is a clash between her approach to life and Bal's non-pragmatic style of life. She accompanies Bal to Bombay and submits to him compromising with the hard reality of life. The fourth category of woman in Jhabvala's fiction is submissive as well as deceptive. Olivia in

*Heat and Dust* submits to Douglas. They are from the same background in all dimensions but she is impulsive and emotional resulting in her elopement with the Nawab. These four types of impulses are revealed in the personality of many women characters in Jhabvala's fiction. Of course, these vary according to the environments, and human beings react to different circumstances in different ways: "a person's behaviour depends not only on the situation in which he finds himself, but also upon the way in which he views himself and what self attitude he has."[7] So the same person can behave in different ways at different times. A passive and submissive character can become assertive and aggressive or vice versa. Indeed, "no character can be fully judged by his/her behaviour at a particular place or time as human behaviour is not static. It is always in a flux."[8]

Jhabvala's female protagonists thus, behave in different ways at different times. Indu, Sarla Devi, Gulab, Judy and Olivia behave in divergent ways with the force of their impulses but all of them suffer from marital disintegration. For Indu there is disharmony for some time but as a pregnant woman she returns to her husband's house. Prem cleverly manages the restoration of harmony. Jhabvala's Sarla Devi, an idealist to the core, clashes with Gulzari Lal who is a materialist to the core. Therefore, dissonance takes the shape of divorce and leaves no scope for reconciliation. Gulab and Esmond face the predicament born out of cross-cultural marriages. Gulab leaves the house without taking divorce and goes to her parents. Judy in *A Backward Place* is from the West but she compromises with the desires of Bal and avoids any separation. Olivia in *Heat and Dust*, with her sensuousness, becomes responsible for breaking the domestic harmony. Jhabvala excels in presenting incongruities of human character and situation into dramatic action. These incongruities have social, marital, familial and cultural implications and consequently become the source of marital dissonance.

Anita Desai is deeply concerned with the inner world of human beings and their turmoils and upheavals in their family affairs and social environment. The theme of marital dissonance and inharmonious man-woman relations figure mostly in her novels taken here for study. For example, Maya and Gautama in *Cry, the Peacock*, Monisha and Jiban in *Voices in the City*, Sita and Raman in *Where Shall We Go This Summer?*, Mrs. Nanda Kaul and Mr. Kaul in *Fire on the Mountain,* and Sarla and Deven in *In Custody* are locked up in unhappy wedlocks.

Desai has tried to introduce a modern psychological vein and project a sensibility generally not encountered in other Indian English women writers of fiction. A study of her novels reveals three important areas of excellence—characterisation, theme and structure. Her style is unique in its own way and is beautifully suited to the intrinsic needs of her art. The theme of marital dissonance is drawn so neatly that each novel becomes a distinctive world in miniature. Maya might not have been an introvert and a killer, Monisha a self-destroyer, or Nanda Kaul an exile among the crowd, had they got the sympathetic attention of their husbands. "These rebel-victims are not the outcome of an eccentric vision of the author but they are indicative of the emergence of this disquieting stance which modern literature stands to project."[9] Another important aspect which is emphasized is the carelessness of the husbands very often described as the prose of life. Desai hints that cold light of reason may help one passing the time but cannot solve the problem of marital dissonance. Gautama, Jiban and Mr. Kaul, therefore, have failed to satisfy their women. Desai, by projecting women comparatively in sober roles, tries to focus on their aggressiveness and submissiveness. Sita and Sarla at last reconcile to the hard reality of life.

As a matter of fact, Desai dislikes aggressive attitude in women but in spite of her unwillingness at times she creates characters like Maya, Monisha and Sita. She seems to point out that the role of women changes according to the situation and it is up to men to understand them and avoid marital dissonance.

To sum up, Desai has given primary importance to the individual. It is significant to note that in her novels no role or reaction—whether it be violent or silent, subdued or emphasized—has gone unnoticed. An attempt to highlight an important aspect of modern thought and civilization related to psychoanalysis has been made in her works. Needless to say, the novels taken for study here strike a note of warning without being didactic or moralistic; her works clearly suggest that modern life with all its spectacular achievement and progress, is doomed to disorder, dissonance, dissolution and destruction unless it considers and nourishes the tender feelings of the women who form the nucleus of any society. Herein lies the most spectacular and important achievement that adds a new dimension to Desai's literary work and gives her a significant place in the realm of Indian women's fiction.

Desai moves very cautiously towards the creation of self-conscious women characters. She is yet to take the plunge to create the staunch believers of the new value system who can dare question the established norms degrading women. Her task is difficult because a woman's psyche is governed by different principles and she has to create "probable" characters. Her women continue to be second class citizens of our society. Yet one cannot overlook her achievement as she has made women aware of man's unjust stance. The new woman is in her embryonic stage and one can hope to see her birth in Anita Desai's new imaginative efforts.

An important aspect of woman that features in the authors is that of mother, mother-in-law and daughter-in-law. In Jhabvala's fiction, the Indian wife is a silent suffering woman like Indu in *The Householder*. As a mother-in-law, she is never willing to allow the wife to gain a hold on the feelings of her son. The young bride who finds the adjustment difficult suffers her bitter and unhappy frustrations silently. The involvement of mother in *Esmond in India* makes daughter Gulab realize that her son Ravi should be brought up in the Eastern way and not in the Western way. Similarly, we find the involvement of mother-in-law in Desai's *Voices in the City* where Monisha's mother-in-law dominates the domestic administration and orders the daughter-in-law to massage her legs. That shows how Jiban's mother dictates the terms. Besides this, the aspect of extra-marital relationship is also focussed upon in the works of the authors here. In *Get Ready for Battle*, Kusum controls the household and governs in the absence of Sarla Devi. Shakuntala in *Esmond in India* prevails upon Esmond. Olivia in *Heat and Dust* is so extreme that she elopes with the Nawab once for all. A similar situation of extra-marital relationship that disrupts marital life is found in Desai's *Fire on the Mountain*. Mr. Kaul continues his illegitimate affair with Miss David. Thus we find the projection of the image of mother, mother-in-law and daughter-in-law and the involvement of extra-marital relationship to be identical in both the authors though Jhabvala is the daughter-in-law of India and Desai is the daughter of India.

The portrayal of various characters in the works of Jhabvala and Desai are complementary. Both of them emphasize, from different perspectives, the role of harmonious familial ties. Jhabvala's sociological bearings and Desai's psychological implications with reference to the theme of marital dissonance make their works an engrossing study for those who explore the reality of human happiness in terms of sociological concerns and psychological truths. Whenever there is some snag or an unoiled cog anywhere in the network of wife and husband relationships, uncertainty, disintegration, dissonance surround the protagonists. Moreover, at the present moment, when a cynical could-not-care-less attitude is fast developing to corrode the foundations of marriage, these novels of Jhabvala and Desai can definitely serve as eye-openers. They inspire one to cherish these bonds and maintain their harmony.

The artistic value of the writing of Jhabvala and Anita Desai is validated by their sociological and psychological aims to right the wrongs. These writers seem to believe that the woman's heart is like a fruit which can only prosper in the warm sunshine of love and that love should be showered on the woman by the husband for a harmonious life making the home as the paradise on earth instead of worrying about Heaven after death. They do not consider marriage simply as a ritual; for them it is a kind of concord, it involves adapting and adopting understanding a genuine urge to encourage—mutually—the spirit to continue and the desire to create. Marital dissonance is definitely a reality, a painful disturbing fact of conjugal life, but its causes are rooted in the rigidity of male behaviour and, consequently, in the seemingly abnormal relations of women. Both the writers deserve admiration for such a deep insight into the nature of male-female behaviour—marriage being the medium to verbalize them.

## NOTES

1 Bidulata Choudhury, *Women and Society in the Novels of Anita Desai* (New Delhi: Creative, 1995), p. 2

2 *Ibid.*, p. 5.

3 M.S. Mahale, "Marriage in Jhabvala's Novels," *Indo-Anglian Fiction: Some Perceptions* (New Delhi: Jainsons, 1985), p. 51.

4 K.R. Srinivasa Iyengar, *Indian Writing in English* (New Delhi: Sterling, 1984), p. 455.

5 Bidulata Choudhury, *Women and Society in the Novels of Anita Desai* (New Delhi: Creative, 1995), p. 48.

6 Anna Rutherford and Kristen Peterson, "*Heat and Dust:* Ruth Prawer Jhabvala's Experience of India," *World Literature Written in English*, vol. 15, No. 11 (November 1976), p. 373.

7 B. Kuppuswamy, *An Introduction to Social Psychology* (Bombay: Asia, 1971), p. 351.

8 Ramesh Chadha, "Image of Woman in the Fiction of Jhabvala," in *Indian Women Novelists*, ed. R.K. Dhawan (New Delhi: Prestige, 1993), set II, vol. 5, p. 214.

9 Usha Bande, *The Novels of Anita Desai* (New Delhi: Prestige, 1988), p. 20.